# P UPANISHAD

## Essence and Sanskrit Grammar

Ashwini Kumar Aggarwal

जय गुरुदेव

ISBN13: 978-81-944890-6-1  Paperback Edition
ISBN13: 978-81-944890-7-8  Hardbound Edition
ISBN13: 978-81-944890-8-5  Digital Edition



Title: Prashna Upanishad
SubTitle: Essence and Sanskrit Grammar

Printed and Published by
Devotees of Sri Sri Ravi Shankar Ashram
34 Sunny Enclave, Devigarh Road
Patiala 147001, Punjab, India

https://advaita56.weebly.com/
The Art of Living Centre

https://www.artofliving.org/

15th Jan 2020, Makara Sankranti, Pongal, Magha Pancami
Uttara Phalguni Nakshatra, Shishir Ritu, Uttarayana Starts
Vikram Samvat 2076 Paridhavi, Saka Era 1941 Vikari

1st Edition January 2020

जय गुरुदेव

Dedication

Sri Sri Ravi Shankar

who gave us AUM Meditation as अम् उम् मम्

## Blessing

"OM is the sound that goes all the way from the bottom of the Spine up, up to the top of the Crown… Crown Chakra.

The sound OM has the same frequency as the Earth's rotation.

OM means Peace, Love, Purity, Clarity, Serenity."

Sri Sri Ravi Shankar<br>Bangalore Ashram

Acknowledgements

A joyous Lohri Makara Sankranti soaking in Satsang.

Cover Photo Credits

https://pixabay.com/photos/russian-dolls-matryoshka-nesting-912310/
image by Jacqueline Macou from Pixabay

# Preface

Once an eon something brilliant happens. This brilliance is a galactic birth, the birth of billions of bright stars and majestic minds.

This is such an occasion. Right now it is happening. Beauty is in fashion. Benevolence is showering.

At such time, the intellect expands. Divinity knocks. The mind is open. And the Lord walks in.

| Veda | |
| --- | --- |
| Mantra Verses (Samhita) | Brahmana Verses |
| | Brahmana<br>Aranyaka<br>Upanishad |

Adi Shankaracharya's masterly commentary on eleven Upanishads is the de facto standard for Vedanta. These eleven have been named the principal Upanishads. Though it is said there are 1180 Upanishads written over a period of a thousand years, actual manuscripts available as of now are 108 only.

A chart that lists the eleven Upanishads commented on in detail by Sankara.

| Rigveda | Samaveda | <u>Shukla Yajurveda</u> Krishna Yajurveda | Atharvaveda |
|---|---|---|---|
| Gives the fundamental laws of creation | Gives the intrinsic harmony within creation | Gives the specific design, administrative and governing principles for a family or a nation | Gives the specific ritucharya and dinacharya for an individual |
| **Aitareya** | Kena **Chandogya** | Ishavasya **<u>Brihadaranyaka</u>** Katha Taittiriya Shvetashvatara | **Mandukya** Mundaka Prashna |
| प्रज्ञानम् ब्रह्म | तत् त्वम् असि | अहं ब्रह्म अस्मि | अयम् आत्मा ब्रह्म |

Four great illuminating statements or mahavakyas are listed above with their corresponding Upanishads in **bold**. The Prashna has its very own mahavakya - यच्चित्तस्तेनैष प्राणमायाति प्राणस्तेजसा युक्तः सहात्मना यथासङ्कल्पितं लोकं नयति ॥ 3.10

Remember that Vedic Sanskrit text cannot be literally translated into English. Thoughts form and words sprout in deep meditation when guided by a living master.

<u>Atharva Veda = Atharvaveda Samhita + Atharvaveda Brahmana.</u>
As of today, Samhita portion is available in two recensions, namely Paippalada and Shaunaka. Brahmana portion is available in one recension only, namely Gopatha Brahmana. Prashna is attributed to sage Pippalada and is in the Gopatha Brahmana. Pippalada is the scientist who got it first, while Gopatha is the scientist who made it known to the world. The Samhita portion is the practical aspect, that details how the day's routine should be, what one should wear and when, what not to eat, which ritual to perform and how, when to sleep, etc. The Brahmana portion reflects on it and in the form of a dialogue seeks to answer the profound questions regarding existence that lead to happiness and nirvana.

Mundaka verses are actually in the earlier portion, and in the later portion are the Prashna verses. Thus Prashna contains the complete essence, including that of Mundaka. Prashna Upanishad प्रश्न उपनिषद् gets its name from प्रश्न = Prashna = "a Question".

When
one's mind is peaceful,
the heart is loving,
basic needs are well taken care of,
Then
a question that arises is directly addressed by the Divine, since it is addressed only to the Divine.

# Table of Contents

# Prayer

शान्तिपाठः

ॐ भद्रं कर्णेभिः शृणुयाम देवाः । भद्रं पश्ये माक्षभिर् यजत्राः ।
स्थिरैरङ्गैस् तुष्टुवाꣳ सस्तनूभिः । व्यशेम देवहितं यदायुः ।
स्वस्ति न इन्द्रो वृद्धश्रवाः । स्वस्ति नः पूषा विश्ववेदाः ।
स्वस्ति नस्ताक्ष्यों अरिष्टनेमिः । स्वस्ति नो बृहस्पतिर्दधातु ॥
ॐ शान्तिः शान्तिः शान्तिः ॥

śāntipāṭhaḥ

oṃ bhadraṃ karṇebhiḥ śṛṇuyāma devāḥ | bhadraṃ paśye mākṣabhir yajatrāḥ | sthirairaṅgais tuṣṭuvāꣳ sastanūbhiḥ | vyaśema devahitaṃ yadāyuḥ | svasti na indro vṛddhaśravāḥ | svasti naꣳ pūṣā viśvavedāḥ | svasti nastārkṣyo ariṣṭanemiḥ | svasti no bṛhaspatirdadhātu ‖ oṃ śāntiḥ śāntiḥ śāntiḥ ‖

## Peace Invocation
O Lord!
May our senses be fully functional. May our joints be firm and supple. May our reasoning be without malice. May our desires be for our welfare and for the welfare of the entire neighborhood.

May our conscience be up and awake.
May we let go of rigidity, obstinacy, false notions.

Peace in our heart, in our body and in our environs.

अथ प्रश्न–उपनिषद् (प्रशनोपनिषद्)

atha Praśna Upaniṣad

# Now begins the Praśna

Vowel Sandhi – Guna Sandhi – अ + उ → ओ

प्रश्न + उपनिषद् → प्रश्नोपनिषद् ।

## The Six Seekers

- Sukesha सुकेशा (wonderful hair, well-groomed, avoid dandruff, maintain dress code and personality) the son of भारद्वाजः Bharadvaja.
- Satyakama सत्यकामः (truthful honest dedicated sincere in efforts) the son of शिबिः Shibi.
- Sun-God's grandson सूर्यस्य पौत्रः (resplendent, brilliant, full of the vigor of life, fit as a fiddle) having गर्ग गोत्रः surname Garg.
- Kausalya कौसल्यः (healthy, pleasant and cheerful, peaceful and happy) the son of अश्वलः Ashvala.
- Bhargava भार्गवः, descendent of Bhrigu भृगु गोत्रः (wealthy, resourceful, centered) from विदर्भः Vidarbha-the center of India.
- Kabandhi कबन्धी, the great grandson of कत्यः Katya.

In India, *Garg, Kaushal, Bhargav* are common surnames.

## Qualifications Prerequisites

Respectfulness, Readiness to serve with cheerfulness, Capacity to maintain discipline for one year with frugal lifestyle

# 1st Question by Kabandhi

## How is the Universe sustained?

Universe is sustained by food. It is a principle that operates in creation. There is a food-chain. Food is created, nourishment happens and all beings get sustenance.

## Name and Form = Life and Matter

Name = Life  = Living Matter
Form = Matter = Cosmic Dust
Both are inteconnected and tightly coupled, though we may have only Name and only Form as well. Creation is infinite, the Supreme loves diversity, even though a large part adheres to some law, rare cases cannot be so confined, this Is the Beauty in Diversity.

## Sunlight and Moonlight = Prana and Rayi

## Southern and Northern Pathways

Pleasure and Beyond Pleasure.
The Downward and Upward Currents.

Initially our mother pampers us, with many goodies, and running to our side when we are infants 100s of times a day. When one is young, the neighbors and folks around us are kind and forgiving and benevolent; society rarely enforces laws over children.

These and such moments are collectively called the Southern pathway, or the pleasurable journey, that is naïve, childish forgettable. Even when one grows up, if one continues to behave indulgingly and live in unawareness and intoxication, then Nature steps in to punish by ruining our health, relationships or finances. In the end, one departs regretful, sorrowful, begging pardon.

For some of us, awakening comes early. A Master, or a School, or a Colleague, or some Adventure, turns our path from pleasure to Beyond pleasure.

The moment comes when one no longer craves for pleasure. One is no longer hankering for goodies that have an iOweYou sting. One no longer relishes food that has not been honestly earned. One finds gifts and perks bothersome. One wishes to live sans entanglement. Free in Mind, Light in Heart.

This is known as the Northern pathway. The journey beyond pleasure. The life of discipline, hard work, sincerity, and self-growth.

The Vedic Rishis were seers of a high order. They used simple commonplace words to guide and teach. Many people came to them seeking advice. It was not a seeking, rather people wanted the Master to identify which of their desires was unworthy. They wished the master to stamp approval on the option that was safe and sound. The kind hearted master simply said – This is the Southern pathway,

pleasurable initially and hell in the long run. That is
the Northern pathway, difficult to begin with and not
at all likable to the senses. Yet a path that guarantees
victory in the long run.

For experiencing the truth of the Upward and
Downward play of Prana, one can do Sri Sri's Chakra
Meditation taught in the Advanced Meditation Course
(AMC).

For experiencing and owning these fine movements and
vibrations so that we can well integrate the interplay of
subtle purifying currents, we may join the Sanyam
Course of the Art of Living.

ॐ

सुकेशा च भारद्वाजः शैब्यश्च सत्यकामः सौर्यायणी च गार्ग्यः
कौसल्यश्चाश्वलायनो भार्गवो वैदर्भिः कबन्धी कात्यायनस्ते हैते ब्रह्मपरा
ब्रह्मनिष्ठाः परं ब्रह्मान्वेषमाणा एष ह वै तत्सर्वं वक्ष्यतीति ते ह
समित्पाणयो भगवन्तं पिप्पलादमुपसन्नाः ॥ १.१

oṃ

sukeśā ca bhāradvājaḥ śaibyaśca satyakāmaḥ sauryāyaṇī ca
gārgyaḥ kausalyaścāśvalāyano bhārgavo vaidarbhiḥ
kabandhī kātyāyanaste haite brahmaparā brahmaniṣṭhāḥ
paraṃ brahmānveṣamāṇā eṣa ha vai tatsarvaṃ vakṣyatīti
te ha samitpāṇayo bhagavantaṃ pippalādamupasannāḥ ॥
1.1


पदच्छेदः

सुकेशा च भारद्वाजः शैब्यः च सत्यकामः सौर्यायणी च गार्ग्यः
कौसल्यः च आश्वलायनः भार्गवः वैदर्भिः कबन्धी कात्यायनः ते ह एते
ब्रह्मपराः ब्रह्मनिष्ठाः परं ब्रह्म अन्वेषमाणाः एषः ह वै तत् सर्वं वक्ष्यति
इति ते ह समित्पाणयः भगवन्तं पिप्पलादम् उपसन्नाः ॥


अन्वयः

भारद्वाजः <sup>m1/1</sup> सुकेशा<sup>m1/1</sup> (Bharadvaja's son) Bhāradvaja
(also known as) Sukeśā, च <sup>0</sup>and

शैब्यः <sup>m1/1</sup> सत्यकामः <sup>m1/1</sup> (Śibi's son) Śaibya (also known
as) Satyakāma, च <sup>0</sup> and

सौर्यायणी <sup>m1/1</sup> गार्ग्यः <sup>m1/1</sup> (grandson of Surya the Sun-
god) Sauryāyaṇī (also known as) Gārgya, च <sup>0</sup> and

आश्वलायनः <sup>m1/1</sup> कौसल्यः <sup>m1/1</sup> (Aśvalāya's son) Āśvalāyan (also known as) Kausalya, च <sup>0</sup> and

वैदर्भिः <sup>m1/1</sup> भार्गवः <sup>m1/1</sup> (the one from the land of Vidarbha) Vaidarbhi (also known as) Bhārgava,

कात्यायनः <sup>m1/1</sup> कबन्धी <sup>m1/1</sup> (Katya's great grandson) Kātyāyana (also known as) Kabandhī,

ते <sup>m1/3</sup> ह <sup>0</sup> Verily they;

एते <sup>m1/3</sup> ब्रह्मपराः <sup>m1/3</sup> ब्रह्मनिष्ठाः <sup>m1/3</sup> those who were seeking Brahman and who were earnestly practicing their attainment for Brahman,

परं <sup>n1/1</sup> ब्रह्म <sup>n1/1</sup> अन्वेषमाणाः <sup>PrPA m1/3</sup> in that seeking for the Ultimate Brahman,

एषः <sup>m1/1</sup> ह <sup>0</sup> वै <sup>0</sup> This surely

तत् <sup>n1/1</sup> सर्वं <sup>m1/1</sup> वक्ष्यति <sup>लृट् iii/1</sup> "It all he shall expound"

इति <sup>0</sup> thus (thinking),

ते <sup>m1/3</sup> ह <sup>0</sup> समित्पाणयः <sup>m1/3</sup> They-once upon a time-with due reverence, sincerity, and willingness to serve,

भगवन्तं <sup>m2/1</sup> पिप्पलादम् <sup>m2/1</sup> उपसन्नाः <sup>PPP m1/3</sup> ॥

approached the Sage Pippalada.


**1.1** The number 6 wants to ascend to 7. Symbolically 7 is the highest state, as the sahasrara chakra. Or 7 is the maximum no of items, objectives or milestones.

A method of quality control is named Six sigma. An earthquake of 6 magnitude is considered very strong.

In cricket, a popular sport today, there are 6 balls in an over and 6 runs is the maximum hit off a ball. After 6 days of working we earn a weekend.

Similarly 6 players make a team in volleyball. A honeycomb is a hexagon. In IELTS, a score of 6 is the minimum requirement to apply to a top school. Mathematically 6 is a perfect number. And in Yoga, Vedanta and fitness classes, the 6th sense is a prized - to be polished - faculty.

So this Upanishad is in the form of a dialog between 6 disciples and a Master. The 6 disciples do not mean six physical bodies. Rather it points to the fact that only after one has crossed 6 milestones or 6 levels does one possess enough qualification to aspire for the ultimate.

In fact it also points to the basic principle in operation in a human socio-economic set-up. To attain to the top rung in any civil or military or spiritual context, advancing 6 levels is needed.

Another quality for the aspirant consists of साधन–चतुष्टय the 4 personality traits:

> 1) A trustful, respectful, discriminating attitude. विवेकः Viveka.

> 2) Showing restraint or dispassion in matters unconnected to the job. Not overstepping one's work domain. वैराग्यं Vairagya.

3) A willingness and endurance to serve whole-heartedly for a length of time, e.g. a year or two years. षट् सम्पत्तिः Shat Sampatti.

4) A desire to learn, evolve, become more useful. मुमुक्षुत्वं Mumukshutva.

So when an aspirant has cleared 6 stages in life and his personality reflects these 4 traits, he is qualified to enter the pure Brahman space.

6 such seekers got admission to Stanford, or IIT Bombay, or the Art of Living Ashram. They were asked to prove their mettle and display their capabilities by going through a rigorous orientation program for 12 months. The program also tested whether company policy and institute ground rules were properly adhered to by the entrants.

तान् ह स ऋषिरुवाच भूय एव तपसा ब्रह्मचर्येण श्रद्धया संवत्सरं संवत्स्यथ यथाकामं प्रश्नान् पृच्छत यदि विज्ञास्यामः सर्वं ह वो वक्ष्याम इति ॥ १.२

tān ha sa ṛṣiruvāca bhūya eva tapasā brahmacaryeṇa śraddhayā saṃvatsaraṃ saṃvatsyatha yathākāmaṃ praśnān pṛcchata yadi vijñāsyāmaḥ sarvaṃ ha vo vakṣyāma iti ॥ 1.2

तान् to them ह *(with emotion)* सः he ऋषिः the Master उवाच said भूयः additionally एव only तपसा by great discipline ब्रह्मचर्येण by balance in routine श्रद्धया by faith संवत्सरं for a year संवत्स्यथ maintain yourself यथाकामं then as desired प्रश्नान् questions पृच्छत you may ask यदि if विज्ञास्यामः answers are known to us सर्वं all ह surely वः to you all वक्ष्यामः we shall expound इति

---

अथ कबन्धी कात्यायन उपेत्य पप्रच्छ ।
भगवन् कुतो ह वा इमाः प्रजाः प्रजायन्त इति ॥ १.३

atha kabandhī kātyāyana upetya papraccha |
bhagavan kuto ha vā imāḥ prajāḥ prajāyanta iti ॥ 1.3

अथ after a year had passed कबन्धी Kabandhin कात्यायनः the great grandson of Katya उपेत्य having presented himself पप्रच्छ । specifically asked. भगवन् O Lord कुतः whence ह वै *(displaying lots of intense emotion)* इमाः these प्रजाः diverse creatures प्रजायन्ते come into being इति ॥

कबन्धी m1/1 *from stem* कबन्धिन् । वै इमाः = वा इमाः *(due to ayava sandhi and subsequently elision sandhi)*

**1.2** No promises were made, nor any hope raising by flowery language.

The gurukul had an excellent canteen that served sufficient and nutritious food at specific meal times, there were lots of physically demanding chores and running about to keep them in peak fitness, the living quarters were Spartan to prevent laziness, sloth and indulgence. The head very professionally advised them to get on with their tasks, and not to disturb him till their orientation was over.

---

**1.3** Ka-Bandhin, the one who feels trapped, "What for this Trap?", and is always seeking to be free, was the first to complete his orientation process successfully. He ran to the Master, all quivering, and with head bowed and hands folded, stood before him.

When the great Master kindly acknowledged his presence, choosing his words carefully, Ka-Bandhi enquired. "O Great One, why do so many men and beasts and creatures take birth? Who is responsible for their sustenance? Does anyone bother to ensure their well-being?

It seems from nothing the flora and fauna is sprouting, bees and bacteria are emanating, then how is it possible that they shall find joy? What ensures that man shall experience peace? How does anyone obtain satisfaction?

तस्मै स होवाच प्रजाकामो वै प्रजापतिः स तपोऽतप्यत स तपस्
तप्त्वा स मिथुनमुत्पादयते । रयिं च प्राणं चेत्येतौ मे बहुधा प्रजाः
करिष्यत इति ॥ १.४

tasmai sa hovāca prajākāmo vai prajāpatiḥ sa tapo'tapyata
sa tapas taptvā sa mithunamutpādayate | rayiṃ ca prāṇaṃ
cetyetau me bahudhā prajāḥ kariṣyata iti ॥ 1.4

तस्मै to him सः he (the master) ह gracefully उवाच
replied,
प्रजाकामः desirous of diversity वै indeed प्रजापतिः the
Creator सः he तपः intense austerity अतप्यत did,
सः he तपः deep meditation तप्त्वा having done,
सः he मिथुनम् with love making उत्पादयते । produced,

रयिं cosmic dust च and प्राणं life force.

च and इति with them एतौ both together मे my बहुधा
multifold प्रजाः diversity करिष्यतः they shall create
इति ॥ so the story goes.

**1.4** The Master was not to be thwarted so easily. He got down to basic biology, and simply said - of course all creatures take birth due to the intercourse of the male and female of their species. Naturally they grow by leaps and bounds by the simple laws of mathematical division and multiplication.

To make the discussion technical and professional, the Master continued - you may consider the male sperm as a continuous moving energy beam. The female egg can be thought of as a body of matter that is impregnated and infused with life by the male energy beam falling on it.

Now as to the question of why does the energy interact with matter, the answer is ridiculously simple. For enjoyment, entertainment, and self-protection. It is for this reason we all strive to expand our holdings, stock, land and possessions.

It gives man much pleasure when his progeny increases and his wealth multiplies.

So also nature seeks to produce a variety and diversity of phenomena. By altering the strength, direction, and interplay of its energies, mother nature succeeds in spawning an amazing tapestry of all sorts of beings and matter, animate and inanimate.

And we can imagine mother nature to be united with

a fatherly force, to keep the equation simple and the theory digestible.

To say that someone did something for oneself, be it profit, entertainment or pleasure, is kind of the most acceptable legal statement for a jury or judge to decide the case and put an end to further enquiry.

This is how the Master taught the boy biology, math, geography, history and law.

Obviously "the Ultimate" could not be learnt directly, but it could be catalyzed by learning everything else perfectly.

Sooner or later the seed of infinity would sprout, and the boy would attain enlightenment.

आदित्यो ह वै प्राणो रयिरेव चन्द्रमा रयिर्वा एतत् सर्वं यन्मूर्तं चामूर्तं च
तस्मान्मूर्तिरेव रयिः ॥ १.५

ādityo ha vai prāṇo rayireva candramā rayirvā etat sarvaṃ
yanmūrtaṃ cāmūrtaṃ ca tasmānmūrtireva rayiḥ ॥ 1.5

आदित्यः the Sun ह वै is certainly प्राणः the Life force
रयिः the Cosmic Dust एव likewise चन्द्रमा the Moon,

रयिः Cosmic Dust वै alone एतत् this सर्वं all यत् what
मूर्तं with form च and अमूर्तं formless,

च and तस्मात् hence मूर्तिः a form एव only रयिः ॥
matter (is).

**1.5** To make the discourse practical and interesting, and the concept clear; the Master gave the analogy of the Sun and the Moon. Just as the fiery sun makes us all wake up and go about our chores, and the beautiful moon provides much needed soothing rest and time for entertainment, so does mother nature synchronize both work and play.

Seemingly after birth, the father's role vanishes, the mother gets to do many tasks and provide various bells and whistles. So does Brahman recede into the background. The young children interact and grow up learning from mother, other relatives, society and environment. All of which is supposedly supervised and directed by mother's will.

अथादित्य उदयन् यत् प्राचीं दिशं प्रविशति तेन प्राच्यान् प्राणान्
रश्मिषु सन्निधत्ते । यद् दक्षिणां यत् प्रतीचीं यदुदीचीं यदधो यदूर्ध्वं
यदन्तरा दिशो यत्सर्वं प्रकाशयति तेन सर्वान् प्राणान् रश्मिषु सन्निधत्ते
॥ १.६

athāditya udayan yat prācīṃ diśam praviśati tena prācyān
prāṇān raśmiṣu sannidhatte | yad dakṣiṇāṃ yat pratīcīṃ
yadudīcīṃ yadadho yadūrdhvaṃ yadantarā diśo yatsarvaṃ
prakāśayati tena sarvān prāṇān raśmiṣu sannidhatte ||  1.6

अथ Then आदित्यः the Sun उदयन् rising यत् from प्राचीं
the eastern दिशं direction प्रविशति comes up,

तेन due to that प्राच्यान् eastern,
प्राणान् the life forces रश्मिषु in the sunrays सन्निधत्ते ।
are held.

यत् that दक्षिणां southern यत् that प्रतीचीं western यत्
that उदीचीं northern यत् that अधः below यत् that ऊर्ध्वं
above यत् that अन्तरा intervening दिशः space यत् that
सर्वं all प्रकाशयति is lighted up,

तेन by that सर्वान् all प्राणान् living beings रश्मिषु due to
the sunrays सन्निधत्ते ॥ get enlivened.

**1.6** Of course the brilliance is seen far and wide. Surely world champions are hailed in every nook and corner. Light travels quickly to all the four quarters, it's principles of reflection, refraction, linear motion, diffraction, diffusion, dispersion are all taught to the budding student.

And why does physics play such an elementary role? Why do all inventors, creators, and entrepreneurs emphasize the physical principles? It is something visible, interactable, and transactional. Entire economy of a company or country is based on getting the physics right. Product must be appealing, aesthetic, pleasing. So much emphasis on looks, texture, color. Almost all processed foods nowadays get a dose of coloring (artificial), even drugs and raw fruits, spices and vegetables get painted. For any home or office, the interior design is big business, it should have great color combination. Latest the automobile or gadget, funkier the colors. Dress code, fabric, machine or fashion is all about satisfying the eye.

The Master deftly explains the importance of eye, eyesight, and inner vision by drawing parallel to the glory of the sunlight and how sunRays illumine all corners of the globe.

And in the process teaches physics, thermodynamics, kinetics, also optics, communications, and importance of sunlight in life.

स एष वैश्वानरो विश्वरूपः प्राणोऽग्निरुदयते ।
तदेतद् ऋचाऽभ्युक्तम् ॥ १.७

sa eṣa vaiśvānaro viśvarūpaḥ prāṇo'gnirudayate |
tadetad ṛcā'bhyuktam ॥ 1.7


सः he एषः this,
वैश्वानरः the cosmic man विश्वरूपः the cosmic form
प्राणः the life अग्निः the fire,
उदयते । he rises forth.


तत् that (fact) एतत् this ऋचा verse अभ्युक्तम् ॥ states.

**1.7** The Master goes on to teach the amazing use of fire in life. Forging, manufacturing, welding, cutting, molding, ignition, cooking. Almost no human activity proceeds without the direct use of fire. Even worship has a flame, a diya, agarbatti, aarti. All festivals and celebrations have candle lights and exorbitant display of lights and fireworks. Weddings don't happen without the fire ritual.

Movement of any kind, any motor vehicle is impossible without a spark.

Involuntary functions of the body, nervous system, etc. are electric in nature, and digestion cannot proceed without a strong jathar Agni - digestive fire in the stomach.

No mobile phone, laptop, or gadget can work without electricity or battery charge. Electric energy is fast replacing combustion fuel, as evident in the highly successful Tesla Motor vehicles of Elon Musk and home solar panels. Germany is powering entire cities on solar power, the world is following suit.

विश्वरूपं हरिणं जातवेदसं परायणं ज्योतिरेकं तपन्तम् ।
सहस्ररश्मिः शतधा वर्तमानः प्राणः प्रजानामुदयत्येष सूर्यः ॥ १.८
viśvarūpaṃ hariṇaṃ jātavedasaṃ parāyaṇaṃ jyotirekaṃ
tapantam | sahasraraśmiḥ śatadhā vartamānaḥ prāṇaḥ
prajānāmudayatyeṣa sūryaḥ ॥ 1.8

विश्वरूपं the universal form हरिणं tawny yellow
जातवेदसं origin for the word परायणं the basis of
speech ज्योतिः the light एकं the one तपन्तम् ।
effulgent.


सहस्ररश्मिः with a thousand rays शतधा in a hundred
ways,
वर्तमानः presently प्राणः the life प्रजानाम् of all creatures
उदयति sparks,
एषः this सूर्यः ॥ Sun.

$1.8$ Even our brain impulses are electric in nature as seen in neural activity and all thoughts arise from the sparking of 16 neurons.

Nerves are carriers of electric packet information, and the least understood of all anatomical parts.

Gold and Silver are highly prized, and are used as the currency for economic activity as well.

Every home, office, motorway, or township functions due to proper lighting and stable power supply.

Fire and its quality of light and heat that propels and causes movement, all is to be properly studied, harnessed, and made use of.

The master also emphasizes rising up at dawn and greeting the sun, and gazing lovingly at the sunset, meditating at these times.

संवत्सरो वै प्रजापतिस्तस्यायने दक्षिणं चोत्तरं च । तद्ये ह वै तदिष्टापूर्तं कृतमित्युपासते । ते चान्द्रमसमेव लोकमभिजयन्ते । त एव पुनरावर्तन्ते तस्मादेते ऋषयः प्रजाकामा दक्षिणं प्रतिपद्यन्ते । एष ह वै रयिर्यः पितृयाणः ॥ १.९

saṃvatsaro vai prajāpatistasyāyane dakṣiṇaṃ cottaraṃ ca | tadye ha vai tadiṣṭāpūrte kṛtamityupāsate |  te cāndramasameva lokamabhijayante |  ta eva punarāvartante tasmādete ṛṣayaḥ prajākāmā dakṣiṇaṃ pratipadyante |  eṣa ha vai rayiryaḥ pitryāṇaḥ ||  1.9

संवत्सरः in the course of a year वै indeed प्रजापतिः the Lord of Creatures तस्य his अयने travels दक्षिणं the southern path च and उत्तरं the northern path च ।

तत् thus ये those ह वै *(emphatically)* तत् that इष्टापूर्तं in the fulfilment of worldly desire कृतम् act इति thus उपासते । are engrossed,
ते they चान्द्रमसम् moon's domain एव only लोकम् planetary system अभिजयन्ते । attain.
ते they एव surely पुनः again आवर्तन्ते return to earth तस्मात् hence एते these ऋषयः great men प्रजाकामाः desirous of many things दक्षिणं southern course प्रतिपद्यन्ते । travel.
एषः it ह वै *(with emphasis in tone)* रयिः a matter यः of one पितृयाणः ॥ strongly attached to earth.

**1.9** Now the Master introduces the concept of Time. Seconds, minutes, hours. Day, week, month, season, year. All based on the movement of the sun. The humble clock, wristwatch or alarm chime, these govern each and every action of man. No smart phone or computer has been invented that does not use a clock processor chip. And none shall be sold if it does not display the time and date. Our waking, eating, working, sleeping all are time dependent. Our education system has the daily period, monthly timetable, and yearly task scheduler.

What exactly is Time? We can think in the fraction of a second, and remember or imagine events and places far separated in Time. Time hangs heavy during sorrow, and flies gaily during joy. Time makes and breaks relationships, officers get thrown out or penalized for not maintaining the time.

For babies and young children time is not of any great relevance. Animals and plants are not so aware or bothered with time. Inanimate objects and things, furniture and walls and flooring, couldn't care less about time.

How Real is Time, and how much should it intrude our lives? The master discussed all such matters, including duty, responsibility, honesty, discipline and regularity in practice. A stich in time saves nine. Nip the evil in the bud. Early to bed early to rise makes a man healthy, wealthy and wise.

अथोत्तरेण तपसा ब्रह्मचर्येण श्रद्धया
विद्ययात्मानमन्विष्यादित्यमभिजयन्ते । एतद्वै
प्राणानामायतनमेतदमृतमभयमेतत् परायणमेतस्मान्न पुनरावर्तन्त
इत्येष निरोधः। तदेष श्लोकः ॥ १.१०

athottareṇa tapasā brahmacaryeṇa śraddhayā
vidyayātmānamanviṣyādityamabhijayante | etadvai
prāṇānāmāyatanametadamṛtamabhayametat
parāyaṇametasmānna punarāvartanta ityeṣa nirodhaḥ|
tadeṣa ślokaḥ ॥ 1.10

अथ but then उत्तरेण traversing the other path
(northern) तपसा by great discipline ब्रह्मचर्येण by
wholesome living श्रद्धया by faith विद्यया by astute
discernment आत्मानम् soul अन्विष्य having sought
आदित्यम् sun's galactic domain अभिजयन्ते । attain.

एतत् this वै *(said with tonal emphasis)* प्राणानाम् of
lives आयतनम् the super abode (is),
एतत् it अमृतम् the nectar अभयम् the fearlessness (is),
एतत् it परायणम् traversing एतस्मात् due to it न not पुनः
again आवर्तन्ते attach to worldly matters,
इति thus एषः this निरोधः। the final aim.

तत् एषः श्लोकः ॥ that this verse (guarantees).

$1.10$ Followers of time discipline have much to look forward to and rejoice. Their happy moments, eureka phases and "we did it" exultations far outnumber those peoples who behave callous w.r.t. time.

Frequently we have heard the phrase in sport - he sweet times the ball, his timing is perfect. And in all running or swimming or cycling or racing contests, the man who has the best time wins.

Importance of time has been highlighted. Tributes are paid to those who live according to the season and occasion. This is what makes a well-groomed personality that is respected by all.

Timing is inbuilt in our para-sympathetic systems. Heartbeat, hormone release, digestion all run on time for a fit person. Such a person performs well in the world and is regarded as a pillar of society, a model citizen worth emulating.

Even celestial bodies, the sun and moon, have a rhythm in their movement. We all know at what time the sun will rise and set.

Dance, Orchestra, Symphony, Choir, time lends grace to all, great timing is what makes them extraordinary.

The disciple is given no chance of not incorporating timeliness in life. Planning, programming, goal setting, prioritizing, making any event a success requires meticulous adherence to time.

And what of those who have a respect for time and timeliness? This Upanishad verse says -

- They are the real champions.
- They are the most honored.
- Their health and fitness is superior since their breath is unhurried.
- They have no fear, nor any guilt. Untimeliness and procrastination become the biggest source of deep-rooted self-blame, which they never fall prey to.
- Their presence is valued, much sought for.
- Whoever seeks to emulate them also crosses over the shores of suffering.

This is the central teaching. This is a fundamental rule to incorporate in life.

पञ्चपादं पितरं द्वादशाकृतिं दिव आहुः परे अर्धे पुरीषिणम् ।
अथेमे अन्य उ परे विचक्षणं सप्तचक्रे षडर आहुरर्पितमिति ॥ १.११
pañcapādaṃ pitaraṃ dvādaśākṛtiṃ diva āhuḥ pare ardhe
purīṣiṇam | atheme anya u pare vicakṣaṇaṃ saptacakre
ṣaḍara āhurarpitamiti ॥ 1.11

पञ्चपादं fivefold attributes पितरं the father द्वादशाकृतिं twelvefold virtues दिवः the heavenly light आहुः the wisemen say
परे far beyond अर्धे in the cosmic plane पुरीषिणम् । watery.

अथ but then इमे these अन्ये others उ assert परे far beyond विचक्षणं the omniscient सप्तचक्रे of seven wheels षडरे of six spokes आहुः the saying of sages goes अर्पितम् situated इति ॥ thus.

**1.11** Summer Winter Monsoon Autumn and Spring - fivefold is the time planned to aid each soul's temperament. Within the five seasons are the twelve months proportioned, so that man may seek to spend his days wisely and maximize his time in creative endeavors.

Each founding father of a successful organization rotates his employees, chooses his company locations, and shares his wisdom equally amongst his upper echelon executives.

Further, the time has been divided into 7 days in a week for all types of works, jobs, offices and schools, with 6 days of mandatory attendance. This system of time has gotten unqualified approval throughout the ages.

All quarters including the military have sought to give a breather or time for introspection and rejuvenation, to staff and students as the weekly holiday.

मासो वै प्रजापतिस्तस्य कृष्णपक्ष एव रयिः शुक्लः प्राणस्तस्मादेते
ऋषयः शुक्ल इष्टं कुर्वन्तीतर इतरस्मिन् ॥ १.१२

māso vai prajāpatistasya kṛṣṇapakṣa eva rayiḥ śuklaḥ
prāṇastasmādete ṛṣayaḥ śukla iṣṭaṃ kurvantītara itarasmin
॥ 1.12

मासः a month long वै indeed प्रजापतिः the Lord of
Creatures (ordains),
तस्य his कृष्णपक्षः waning fortnight एव only रयिः
matter शुक्लः waxing fortnight प्राणः life,

तस्मात् hence एते these ऋषयः great men शुक्लः waxing
fortnight इष्टं desirous works कुर्वन्ति endeavor to
complete इतरे while others इतरस्मिन् ॥ use the other
(fortnight).

**1.12** Months have been divided into fortnights, specially taking into consideration the waxing and the waning moon. The waning moon fortnight is more suited to the feminine qualities, while the waxing moon fortnight favors masculine traits.

This simply means that each soul has a mix of the tender feminine virtues - grace, emotional bonding, teamwork, flexibility, sensitivity; and the assertive masculine virtues - clarity, focus, mission completion, endurance, bravery. These phases of the moon, viz. The dark fortnight is especially suited to enhancing feminine virtues, while the bright fortnight is more helpful in nurturing masculine traits. The energy content of the moonlight has been studied and analyzed in depth by the Master, who then trains disciples according to which traits of theirs need polishing.

Medical science has progressed to the extent whereby the effects of the new moon and the full moon on the mind have been understood. Also the scientists have observed the beneficial effects of fasting on ekadashi or the 11th day of the moon's cycle. Many agriculturists and farmers are beginning to incorporate the age old wisdom of sowing, harvesting, and rotating crop cycles as per the phases of the moon.

The nutritional quality of herbs, fruits, and vegetables has been found to be greatly affected by moonlight. Some exotic and rare flowers bloom only at night during the moonlight. Some potent formulations, e.g. making kheer on the full moon night of Sharad Poornima, has become a patent ritual considering its confirmed benefits.

अहोरात्रो वै प्रजापतिस्तस्याहरेव प्राणो रात्रिरेव रयिः । प्राणं वा एते प्रस्कन्दन्ति ये दिवा रत्या संयुज्यन्ते ब्रह्मचर्यमेव तद्यद्रात्रौ रत्या संयुज्यन्ते ॥ १.१३

ahorātro vai prajāpatistasyāhareva prāṇo rātrireva rayiḥ |
prāṇaṃ vā ete praskandanti ye divā ratyā saṃyujyante
brahmacaryameva tadyadrātrau ratyā saṃyujyante ||  1.13


अहोरात्रः Day and Night वै it is said प्रजापतिः the Lord तस्य his अहः day एव similar to प्राणः movement earning रात्रिः night एव likewise रयिः । rest enjoying. प्राणं stamina वै surely एते they प्रस्कन्दन्ति dissipate ये who all दिवा during daytime रत्या desiring love संयुज्यन्ते unite in embrace,
ब्रह्मचर्यम् wholesome एव certainly तत् that (love) यत् which रात्रौ during nighttime रत्या for desiring each other संयुज्यन्ते ॥ has intercourse.

## Can we make love anytime?

The master who has a thorough understanding of anatomy, our body's internal design, and the physiological processes predominant during daylight and nighttime, has a simple answer.
Cohabitation makes sense during nighttime since
- that will protect the body,
- maintain one's immunity, and
- be certainly more enjoyable in the ambient conditions prevailing during the night.

$1.13$ And may we salute the day, and pay our respects to the night too, for each has been designed by the Lord for distinctly different activities, to match the design of our anatomy and our brain. Eyesight is supremely connected to sunlight, so also the Vitamin D needed by the body. A regular dose of sunlight will accordingly maintain our vision and strength. Watching the stars and the moonlight, gazing at the dawn and the sunset, empowers us in many ways. These cosmic energies intimately impinge on the body and the mind.

A further point to note is the importance of acts to be done in daytime and in nighttime. The act of copulation is expressly to be done in seclusion, considering it to be most intimate and affecting the brain and physiology greatly. Nighttime or the soft moonlight is much more conducive for physical intimacy as it closely matches the energy spectrum of the brain and biorhythm of the body. This helps in maintaining body fluid balance. Conjugal union at night alone keeps one fit physically, keeps one's emotions healthy, and prevents one's senses from straying unduly.

This information is based on time-tested medical principles of human anatomy, physiology, and psychology. Thus the Upanishad gives clear guidelines to couples for health and happiness in married life, and also for begetting robust children.

अन्नं वै प्रजापतिस्ततो ह वै तद्रेतस्तस्मादिमाः प्रजाः प्रजायन्त इति ॥
१.१४

annaṃ vai prajāpatistato ha vai tadretastasmādimāḥ
prajāḥ prajāyanta iti ॥  1.14

अन्नं food वै certainly प्रजापतिः (is) the Lord of all,

ततः due to it ह वै *(spoken with emphasis)* तत् the
रेतः life generating semen,

तस्मात् from that इमाः these प्रजाः diverse creatures
प्रजायन्ते get life इति ॥

**1.14** Food - good, fresh, nutritious food that gels with your system. Eat such foodstuffs regularly. Eat with respect, honor, and gratefulness. Get proper advice regarding diet. Have the judicious mix of carbohydrates, proteins, vitamins, minerals, fiber from natural foods itself. The Rishi says naturally grown items are compatible with the human system. Eating pills and vitamins is not of much use, since there is only a slim chance that your system can process it.

The presence of sunlight and moonlight, and the appropriate temperature, humidity, pressure, all of these along with the natural soil is what makes the proteins and vitamins digestible - Agreeable to the muscles, bones and nerves - Satiating to the soul. The stuff nature grows no factory can grow. Wait till you get an Android body before you start eating factory made chemicals.

And the story doesn't end here. Sooner or later you might marry. And likely have a baby. Do you have any clue at all as to how a baby is made? Can factories make babies. Not just yet. Prevent continuous contract with the medics and lifelong illnesses.

The Rishi clearly says in this verse, for babies to be born error free, illness free, cheerful, healthy and strong, please eat nature's bounty farm fresh.

तद्ये ह वै तत्प्रजापतिव्रतं चरन्ति ते मिथुनमुत्पादयन्ते ।
तेषामेवैष ब्रह्मलोको येषां तपो ब्रह्मचर्यं येषु सत्यं प्रतिष्ठितम् ॥ १.१५

tadye ha vai tatprajāpativrataṃ caranti te
mithunamutpādayante | teṣāmevaiṣa brahmaloko yeṣāṃ
tapo brahmacaryaṃ yeṣu satyaṃ pratiṣṭhitam ॥ 1.15

तत् hence ये they who ह वै *(emotion in voice)* तत् the
प्रजापतिव्रतं Lord's advice चरन्ति observe,
ते they मिथुनम् a pair by love making उत्पादयन्ते । give
birth to.
तेषाम् for them एव surely एषः the ब्रह्मलोकः great
domain येषां of whose तपः penance ब्रह्मचर्यं
continence येषु in whom सत्यं truth प्रतिष्ठितम् ॥ is well
established.

---

तेषामसौ विरजो ब्रह्मलोको न येषु जिह्ममनृतं न माया चेति ॥ १.१६

teṣāmasau virajo brahmaloko na yeṣu jihmamanṛtaṃ na
māyā ceti ॥ 1.16

तेषाम् for them असौ this (near) विरजः stainless
ब्रह्मलोकः heavenly domain न not येषु in whom जिह्मम्
deceit अनृतं falsehood न not माया ignorance च and
इति ॥ thus.

$1.15$ For sure. It is certain. Those who follow:

- Farm fresh foods in proper quantity and nutritious mix as per recommended diet
- Conjugal union at nighttime only, as it inhibits loss of essential fluids and bone marrow. It Avoids weakening of muscles and nerves, and helps maintain hormonal balance.
- Proper exposure to sunlight. Proper exposure to moonlight. Enough fresh air.

It is guaranteed their married life shall withstand all storms. It is certified their family shall have harmony, hearty emotional bonding, enough excitement and joys. Their progeny shall inherit a value system of Truthfulness, Discipline, Commitment. They shall attain heavenly Bliss in this life.

$1.16$ The Master goes on to enumerate the fruits for those aspirants who prefer to remain unmarried. For those of us who prefer not to raise a family. For those who keep aloof from flirting, follow the principles of honest hard-work, and take out enough time for wholesome exercise. Well such folk too taste the heavenly Bliss. They also taste the joys, excitement, happiness. They also keep robust health. Respect and Stature in society is theirs. Goodwill and Trust enrich their lives.

Thus the Master taught his talented student Reading-Writing-Arithmetic. Personality and Character development. Ethics and Mental toughness in one's workplace. Robust health guidelines. Raising a family and finding Bliss in life.

# 2<sup>nd</sup> Question by Bhargav

**a. Which energies operate inside a Being?**
The 5 elements, the 5 senses, Mind and the Breath.
**b. How are these energies sustained?**
These are all sustained by the Life force we breathe in.
**c. Which of these is the principal energy?**
The Breath is the principal energy.

## Prana = Life Force = Power of Breath

अथ हैनं भार्गवो वैदर्भिः पप्रच्छ । भगवन् कत्येव देवाः प्रजां
विधारयन्ते कतर एतत्प्रकाशयन्ते कः पुनरेषां वरिष्ठ इति ॥ २.१

atha hainaṃ bhārgavo vaidarbhiḥ papraccha |
bhagavan katyeva devāḥ prajāṃ vidhārayante katara
etatprakāśayante kaḥ punareṣāṃ variṣṭha iti ‖ 2.1

अथ Next ह एनं this (fellow) भार्गवः Bhargava वैदर्भिः
the one who hailed from Vidarbha पप्रच्छ ।
decisively queried.

भगवन् O Supreme One! कति How many एव likewise
देवाः the subtle forces प्रजां in the bodies विधारयन्ते
specially take control?
कतरे Of them how many एतत् this (body) प्रकाशयन्ते
animate and make functional?
कः Who पुनः then again एषां of these वरिष्ठः the most
powerful? इति ॥ that's all.

$2.1$ Full of respect and with a sense of awe, the next disciple approached the Master.

He was from Vidarbha or the central Indian Deccan plateau, a region known for harsh weather; and wished to know the science behind luck and good fortune.

He enquired humbly - O Merciful Lord! Please guide us regarding the seemingly unequal distribution of wealth, resources, joys and successes in this world. Who controls what? How does a body get what it needs for existence?

And his final query - which principle is the primary key to man's survival and fitness?

तस्मै स होवाचाकाशो ह वा एष देवो वायुरग्निरापः पृथिवी
वाङ्मनश्चक्षुः श्रोत्रं च । ते प्रकाश्याभिवदन्ति वयमेतद्बाणमवष्टभ्य
विधारयामः ॥ २.२

tasmai sa hovācākāśo ha vā eṣa devo vāyuragnirāpaḥ
pṛthivī vāṅmanaścakṣuḥ śrotraṃ ca | te
prakāśyābhivadanti vayametadbāṇamavaṣṭabhya
vidhārayāmaḥ ॥ 2.2

तस्मै To him सः he ह thus उवाच answered.
आकाशः Space ह वै एषः this देवः energy वायुः air अग्निः
fire आपः water पृथिवी earth वाक् tongue मनः mind
चक्षुः eye श्रोत्रं ear च । and.

ते they प्रकाश्य having animated,
अभिवदन्ति proudly speak,
वयम् we एतत् this बाणम् perishable staff अवष्टभ्य
holding together in one piece विधारयामः ॥ support
and control.

$2.2$ The Master welcomed this strange yet serious question. Willingly he replied - The control of each resource lies with the governing heads of the five elements of which this physical creation is composed of. The five elements are the Space, Air, Fire, Water and Earth. Each element reports to its chief executive officer who is appointed by the Divine Mother.

Additionally the physical creation is infused with intelligence that is commonly known by the sense organs and the reasoning faculty. These all similarly report to their individual presiding officer appointed by the Divine Mother.

The five elements and the processing brain are actually dumb, they simply function as per a set plan with no desire nor notion beyond the obvious. Eating Sleeping Mating Possessing seem to rule everybody. Everyone is trying to look outside and run his affairs based on external appearances. It is hard to find someone who is purifying his innards - developing Kindness Acceptance Belongingness Humility.

And so man keeps spending on the body, senses, and feeding information to the brain. These rule him and by various opportune means signal their importance to him.

तान् वरिष्ठः प्राण उवाच । मा मोहमापद्यथ अहमेवैतत्पञ्चधात्मानं
प्रविभज्यैतद्बाणमवष्टभ्य विधारयामीति तेऽश्रद्दधाना बभूवुः ॥ २.३

tān variṣṭhaḥ prāṇa uvāca | mā mohamāpadyatha ahamevaitatpañcadhātmānaṃ pravibhajyaitadbāṇamavaṣṭabhya vidhārayāmīti te'śraddadhānā babhūvuḥ ॥ 2.3

तान् To them वरिष्ठः the most powerful प्राणः the life force उवाच । said.

मा Be not मोहम् to delusion आपद्यथ succumb,

अहम् I एव alone एतत् this पञ्चधा fivefold आत्मानं human being,

प्रविभज्य having split,

एतत् this बाणम् wooden structure अवष्टभ्य keeping together विधारयाम् maintain and control इति with finality.

ते they (the other subtle forces) अश्रद्दधानाः incredulous बभूवुः <sup>लिट् iii/3</sup> ॥ were.

**2.3** The mightiest of them all - the Breath – counseled,

"Do not spend all your time and money and effort in illusory pursuit".

"In breath is the secret of life, its regulation holds the key to materialistic success and also to spiritual attainment".

"Bodily functions proceed well with deep rhythmic breathing. All mental faculties are kept alert by Pranayama. The 5 major involuntary systems - Respiration, Circulation, Digestion, Excretion and Immunity - are ably supported by various components of the breath".

"You must follow a discipline of Yoga, Pranayama, Walking, and Outdoor activity in fresh air".

Naturally for the busy goal-oriented fellows, this plea fell on deaf ears. It didn't deter the breath, it knew the brave, the noble, the sucessful, and those gifted with divine vision would always have top priority for Pranayama and Meditation.

सोऽभिमानादूर्ध्वमुत्क्रमत इव तस्मिन्नुत्क्रामत्यथेतरे सर्व एवोत्क्रामन्ते
तस्मिंश्च प्रतिष्ठमाने सर्व एव प्रतिष्ठन्ते । तद्यथा मक्षिका
मधुकरराजानमुत्क्रामन्तं सर्व एवोत्क्रामन्ते तस्मिंश्च प्रतिष्ठमाने सर्वा एव
प्रतिष्ठन्त एवं वाङ्मनश्चक्षुः श्रोत्रं च ते प्रीताः प्राणं स्तुन्वन्ति ॥ २.४
so'bhimānādūrdhvamutkramata iva
tasminnutkrāmatyathetare sarva evotkrāmante tasmimśca
pratiṣṭhamāne sarva eva pratiṣṭhante | tadyathā makṣikā
madhukararājānamutkrāmantaṃ sarva evotkrāmante
tasmimśca pratiṣṭhamāne sarvā eva pratiṣṭhanta evaṃ
vāṅmanaścakṣuḥ śrotraṃ ca te prītāḥ prāṇaṃ stunvanti ||
2.4

सः He अभिमानात् due to being offended (by their
vanity) ऊर्ध्वम् got up and set out उत्क्रमते to depart
इव as if,
तस्मिन् in its उत्क्रामति departing अथ then इतरे the
others सर्वे all एव also उत्क्रामन्ते lose consciousness,
तस्मिन् in its च and प्रतिष्ठमाने firmly staying सर्वे all एव
also प्रातिष्ठन्ते । function well.
तत् it यथा just as मक्षिकाः the bees मधुकरराजानम् queen
bee उत्क्रामन्तं taking off सर्वे all एव also उत्क्रामन्ते take
off,
तस्मिन् in its प्रतिष्ठमाने staying put सर्वाः all एव also
प्रतिष्ठन्ते stay put;
एवं hence वाक् tongue मनः mind चक्षुः eye श्रोत्रं च and
ear, ते they प्रीताः having been given proof प्राणं the
life breath स्तुन्वन्ति ॥ glorify.

**2.4** For the pompous, the cruel, or the obstinate, breath becomes shallow, laborious, and feverish. With its fluctuating and miss-timing, the other parameters of the body also become weakened.

Body and senses function well so long as the breath is taken care of. When pranayama is neglected, when outdoor sports and activities are shunned, the body loses immunity and quickly becomes prey to all sorts of illnesses.

Health departs as breath becomes unregulated, life itself bids adieu when the breath leaves.

At such times by a stroke of grace, man renews his friendship with the breath. He steadies himself, re-plans and reprioritizes. He seeks to learn breathing techniques.

Then his speech and intellect start making statements in praise of breath. Then his sight begins to enjoy Yoga, his hearing finds the temple Chants and Bhajans, sounds of Bhastrika and Kriya sweetest.

एषोऽग्निस्तपत्येष सूर्य एष पर्जन्यो मघवानेष वायुः ।
एष पृथिवी रयिर्देवः सदसच्चामृतं च यत् ॥ २.५

eṣo'gnistapatyeṣa sūrya eṣa parjanyo maghavāneṣa vāyuḥ |
eṣa pṛthivī rayirdevaḥ sadasaccāmṛtaṃ ca yat || 2.5

एषः This अग्निः fire तपति lights up
एषः the सूर्यः sun, एषः the पर्जन्यः cloud, मघवान् the
sense controller, एषः the वायुः । air.
एषः This (animates)
पृथिवी the earth रयिः the matter देवः the subtle
energy सत् the real असत् च and the imaginary,
अमृतं च and the eternal यत् ॥ whatever.

**2.5** Suddenly man realizes the truth. What he failed to notice as he kept racing along the raging torrents of social affairs, when he finally got thrown in, it was grace that opened his eyes.

He goes slow and steady, he becomes cultured and reverential, he begins to live when his breathing pattern gets restored to his childhood days.

He notices everything with wonder. The plants and flowers. The bushes and trees. The lakes and rivers. The food and the family members, all seem Divine. The earth and the air become sacred. The fires becomes godly as he participates in Havan and Yagya.

He begins to acknowledge the presence of the almighty. His bitterness and frustration give way to awe and glee.

He senses the divine in peoples and objects. He senses the invisible superior consciousness.

He starts to make his first baby- like innocent movements on the road devoid of lack, on the path that knows no grief.

अरा इव रथनाभौ प्राणे सर्वं प्रतिष्ठितम् ।
ऋचो यजूँषि सामानि यज्ञः क्षत्रं ब्रह्म च ॥ २.६

arā iva rathanābhau prāṇe sarvaṃ pratiṣṭhitam |
ṛco yajūṃṣi sāmāni yajñaḥ kṣatraṃ brahma ca ॥ 2.6

अराः Spokes इव just as रथनाभौ in the chariot wheel
प्राणे in the life force सर्वं everything प्रतिष्ठितम् । is
fitted - ऋचः the cosmos यजूंषि society सामानि
individual यज्ञः endeavor क्षत्रं ruler ब्रह्म च ॥ and
scholar.

---

प्रजापतिश्चरसि गर्भे त्वमेव प्रतिजायसे ।
तुभ्यं प्राण प्रजास्त्विमा बलिं हरन्ति यः प्राणैः प्रतितिष्ठसि ॥ २.७

prajāpatiścarasi garbhe tvameva pratijāyase |
tubhyaṃ prāṇa prajāstvimā baliṃ haranti yaḥ prāṇaiḥ
pratitiṣṭhasi ॥ 2.7

प्रजापतिः The Lord of all beings चरसि moves गर्भे in
the womb त्वम् you (the life breath) एव similarly
प्रतिजायसे । gets infused.
तुभ्यं For thee प्राण O Life breath! प्रजाः the diverse
creatures तु to त्वं you इमाः these बलिं gratefulness
हरन्ति offer यः who प्राणैः by breath प्रतितिष्ठसि ॥ you
maintain.

**2.6** The supreme secret of pranayama dawns. The real truth of life unfolds and it begins to flow meaningfully, just as the car tire glides smoothly when correctly pressurized and kept clean.

Yoga studios and Naturopathy become the fashion. Inner beauty blossoms when ऋचः Family, यजूँषि Work, सामानि Play all make pranayama practice प्रतिष्ठितम् default activity.

**2.7** O Breath! You are just like the great creator. The beating heart confirms thy presence. The moving life-force in the womb signals by means of encouraging kicks - O it's such a delight when a new born greets the air and motherhood is born. You take lungfulls of breath. You make the parents feel as if their likeness has arrived. O what a Blessing to hear you move. To hear the steady pulse.

Everyone respects life. All of nature rejoices when life is born, whether gazelle, calf, cub or flower. Various and multifarious are the celebrations and parties. Living beings are recognized by the moving life energy in them.

देवानामसि वह्नितमः पितॄणां प्रथमा स्वधा ।
ऋषीणां चरितं सत्यमथर्वाङ्गिरसामसि ॥ २.८

devānāmasi vahnitamaḥ pitṛṇāṃ prathamā svadhā |
ṛṣīṇāṃ caritaṃ satyamatharvāṅgirasāmasi ॥ 2.8

देवानाम् Of the subtle energies असि you are वह्नितमः
the fastest पितॄणां of the bodiless beings प्रथमा the
first स्वधा । contact.
ऋषीणां Of the Sages चरितं the pure character सत्यम्
the true strength,
अथर्व–अङ्गिरसाम् of worldly beings the simple joy and
contentment असि ॥ you are.

$2.8$ As we are getting the drift, Prashna Upanishad is stamping the superiority of Breath. Why? So that man learns a Pranayama technique, cultivates it with patience, and then sticks to it by incorporating the Kriya in daily life. Not like bathing or brushing rush jobs, not like fast-food on the go stuffing, not like popping a tablet to get rid of a headache or overcome insomnia. No Sir.

Not in any jerky, time tacky, passionless manner. Nope. That does not qualify as Pranayama. That is not Sudarshan Kriya.

To make the seeker aware of the inner truth is the prime focus of Prashna. It goes on in this verse to extol beautiful aspects of the Life Force.

Prana is वह्नितमः । The fastest, the first to reach the brain. Of all forces and fluids in the body, the prana reaches all cells before anything else. It nourishes, supports, and facilitates each organ best. Hence foremost amongst all Shaktis. Of all energies the greatest.

Of every guest of honor, prana is introduced स्वधा the first प्रथमा, so that it starts to flow in everyone smoothly and proceedings progress without a hitch.

Prana is the Atharvan, अथर्वन् = the simplest, lightest, easiest to regulate. One requiring least effort and expense to make healthy, of all limbs अङ्गिरसाम् and of all sense organs ऋषीणां.

The सत्यं reality and चरितं personality of creation असि you are.

The prime factor in all of creation. The one mark of "he moves thus he is alive and well".

So much emphasis on the Prana in this Upanishad.

- So that it gets firmly etched in the brain.
- It becomes a lifelong habit.
- It evokes awe, respect, belongingness, ownership.
- It becomes invaluable. It becomes priceless.

It achieves the status of:

"COME WHAT MAY,
I SHALL DO MY PRANAYAMA.
I SHALL DO MY SUDARSHAN KRIYA.
I SHALL DO IT SINCERELY. WITH ALL RESPECT. WITH ALL STEPS IN PROPER SEQUENCE. IN COMPLETENESS AS MY MASTER TAUGHT".

इन्द्रस्त्वं प्राण तेजसा रुद्रोऽसि परिरक्षिता ।
त्वमन्तरिक्षे चरसि सूर्यस्त्वं ज्योतिषां पतिः ॥ २.९

indrastvaṃ prāṇa tejasā rudro'si parirakṣitā |
tvamantarikṣe carasi sūryastvaṃ jyotiṣāṃ patiḥ ||  2.9

इन्द्रः Senses Controller त्वं you प्राण O Breath! तेजसा With indomitable effulgence रुद्रः Rudra असि you are परिरक्षिता । the supreme protector.
त्वम् You अन्तरिक्षे in space चरसि animate सूर्यः the Sun, त्वं you ज्योतिषां of all flames पतिः ॥ the light.

यदा त्वमभिवर्षस्यथेमाः प्राण ते प्रजाः ।
आनन्दरूपास्तिष्ठन्ति कामायान्नं भविष्यतीति ॥ २.१०

yadā tvamabhivarṣasyathemāḥ prāṇa te prajāḥ |
ānandarūpāstiṣṭhanti kāmāyannaṃ bhaviṣyatīti ||  2.10

यदा When त्वम् you अभिवर्षसि on all raineth अथ then इमाः these प्राण O Breath! ते they प्रजाः । the creatures,

आनन्दरूपाः in delight तिष्ठन्ति remain hopeful कामाय to their heart's desire अन्नं grain भविष्यति shall be got इति ॥ thus.

**2.9** By your superfine brilliant harness you govern the sense organs - इन्द्रः Indra.

By your flowing nourishing nature रुद्रः Rudra, you strengthen and protect the bodyMind.

You are the steady wind required for incessant combustion and fusion in the heavenly सूर्यः Sun.

You Lord over all flames ज्योतिषां by being their $O_2$ line.

---

**2.10** And the magic happens. Clouds form, air currents transport heavy rain bearing clouds to distant farmlands earnestly seeking, their bellies starving.

Clouds burst, Rains come, and in no time the life giving nectar gives rise to unbridled joy.

Insects humans, otters seals, bears salmon, cows ducks, geese tigers, babies newborns, all experience the thrill of fresh life.

Nature rejoices, there is Bliss all around. Grain is there to gladden the heart, Milk is sweet to nourish the soul. Food a plenty is there for all.

व्रात्यस्त्वं प्राणैकर्षिरत्ता विश्वस्य सत्पतिः ।
वयमाद्यस्य दातारः पिता त्वं मातरिश्व नः ॥ २.११

vrātyastvaṃ prāṇaikarṣirattā viśvasya satpatiḥ |
vayamādyasya dātāraḥ pitā tvaṃ mātariśva naḥ ॥  2.11

व्रात्यः The one not needing initiation त्वं you प्राण O Breath! एकर्षिः the best amongst flames अत्ता the supreme digester विश्वस्य world's सत्पतिः । true companion.

वयम् Weआद्यस्य today and forever shall दातारः care for thee पिता त्वं O Father you! मातरिश्वन् O Motherly one! नः ॥ our.

मातरिश्वन् ᵛ¹/¹ for stem मातरिश्वन् । *However this verse has elided the* नकारः, *a Vedic usage.*

**2.11** O Life force! Thee are uninitiated व्रात्यः, the first light giver एकर्षिः, just as dawn or the first lamp that is lit in the evening. Dawn doesn't have light before, the first lamp that is kindled doesn't have any lamp put on before it, so uninitiated the firstborn, due to whose birth and movement inside the body one senses life for the first time. A baby becomes alive due to the prana, and it experiences all due to the breath.

O Breath! Thee are अत्ता, that which Sparks digestion, that which starts metabolism, that which causes ignition.

O Air! You are Earth's tight hug, as a bride's consort, as a woman's hubby. विश्वस्य सत्पतिः  closest companion.

Waking up we all gulp you in वयं तव आद्यस्य दातारः, we become aware we are alive, we honor thee with Chants, Pranayama, Meditation, Ozone air walks.

O Prana! More than a loving mother मातरिश्वन् त्वं नः पिता, indeed you are our father as well.

या ते तनूर्वाचि प्रतिष्ठिता या श्रोत्रे या च चक्षुषि ।

या च मनसि सन्तता शिवां तां कुरु मोत्क्रमीः ॥ २.१२

yā te tanūrvāci pratiṣṭhitā yā śrotre yā ca cakṣuṣi |

yā ca manasi santatā śivāṃ tāṃ kuru motkramīḥ ॥  2.12

या Which ते that तनूः bodily वाचि in speech प्रतिष्ठिता firmly experienced या which श्रोत्रे in ear या which च चक्षुषि । and in the eyes.

या च and which मनसि in the mind सन्तता causes शिवां peace तां that कुरु you please do, मा do not उत्क्रमीः ॥ exit.

---

प्राणस्येदं वशे सर्वं त्रिदिवे यत् प्रतिष्ठितम् ।

मातेव पुत्रान् रक्षस्व श्रीश्च प्रज्ञां च विधेहि न इति ॥ २.१३

prāṇasyedaṃ vaśe sarvaṃ tridive yat pratiṣṭhitam |

māteva putrān rakṣasva śrīśca prajñāṃ ca vidhehi na iti ॥ 2.13

प्राणस्य Of the breath इदं this वशे under complete control सर्वं all त्रिदिवे in the three planes यत् whatever प्रतिष्ठितम् । exists.

माता इव Just as a mother पुत्रान् the young children रक्षस्व takes full charge similarly श्रीः wealth च and प्रज्ञां intellect च विधेहि particularly grant नः to us इति ॥ that's all.

**2.12** O dear breath! Thou who art firmly flowing in this body and making us hear and see and reason; Make it all auspicious, make us pure, make us divine.

Please do not forsake this body, please do not even consider departure.

Life is so precious, do not quit. The cosmos is made alive by thine presence, keep moving.

**2.13** Verily O Breath! You move in the triumvirate - body, mind, heart. All are dependent upon thee, every human is under your thumb. We all function because of your availability.

Just as a mother protects her young children so do thee ensure our well-being.

O Divine Force! Provide us with sound health, handsome complexion, a sharp brain.

Kindly see to it that we learn to regulate the breath
- so as to live well,
- function ably, and
- rise to stature and respectability in society.

# 3ʳᵈ Question by Kauśal

## a.  What causes the Life force?
The Brahman Shiva consciousness.
## b.  How does it function within the Being?
As five Prana Vayus and five Upaprana Vayus.
## c.  How does it depart?
By means of the Udana Vayu, the Last thought rules.
## d.  What is the cosmic energy?
An intelligent energy that is enlivened by Prana the life force.
## e.  Can it unveil the Soul?
Its awareness through grace helps reveal the Soul.


अथ हैनं कौसल्यश्चाऽऽश्वलायनः पप्रच्छ । भगवन् कुत एष प्राणो जायते कथमायात्यस्मिञ्छरीर आत्मानं वा प्रविभज्य कथं प्रतिष्ठते केनोत्क्रमते कथं बाह्यमभिधत्ते कथमध्यात्ममिति ॥ ३.१

atha hainaṃ kausalyaścā''śvalāyanaḥ papraccha |
bhagavan kuta eṣa prāṇo jāyate kathamāyātyasmiñcharīra ātmānaṃ vā pravibhajya kathaṃ pratiṣṭhate kenotkramate kathaṃ bāhyamabhidhatte kathamadhyātmamiti ॥ 3.1


अथ ह एनं कौसल्यः च आश्वलायनः पप्रच्छ । भगवन् कुतः एषः प्राणः जायते कथम् आयाति अस्मिन् शरीरे आत्मानं वा प्रविभज्य कथं प्रतिष्ठते केन उत्क्रमते कथं बाह्यम् अभिधत्ते कथम् अध्यात्मम् इति ॥

$3.1$ And Now after the earlier quest has been satisfactorily addressed, and the previous thought wave has been quenched.

There is a new surge of fresh current. आश्वलायनः The stormy fleet-footed horse-like कौसल्यः highly observant, all talented wave like energy bursts upon the scene.

In a flurry quest gets tabled, building upon the foundation so far made. 1. How does Life Force = the Prana come into existence? 2. How doth the Breath get tightly coupled to the limp Body? 3. How does it separate into the various functions of respiration, circulation, evacution, and the rest? आत्मानं How does it enter into the flirting of the senses? How causes it dilly-dallying of reason? How brings it upheaval in memory? Why causes it Ego to harden?

केन उत्क्रमते by what mechanism does Prana exit the body?
कथं बाह्यम् अभिधत्ते How does it function externally as cosmic energy to sustain the galaxies and planetary systems?
कथं वा अध्यात्मम् Really how does it get the power to unveil the soul?

तस्मै स होवाचातिप्रश्नान् पृच्छसि ब्रह्मिष्ठोऽसीति तस्मात्तेऽहं ब्रवीमि ॥
३.२

tasmai sa hovācātipraśnān pṛcchasi brahmiṣṭho'sīti
tasmātte'haṃ bravīmi ॥  3.2

तस्मै सः ह उवाच अतिप्रश्नान् पृच्छसि ब्रह्मिष्ठः असि इति तस्मात् ते
अहं ब्रवीमि ॥

# Prana Vayu and Upaprana Vayu

$3.2$ The Master spoke in a tone of caressing benevolence – तस्मै सः ह उवाच

You ask deep fundamental questions. Questions that never occur to the ordinary student. अतिप्रश्नान् पृच्छसि

Much mature yet equally humble art thee. Keen yet sure-footed, bold and incisive, impatient but not awkward your tone. ब्रह्मिष्ठः असि

Hence I shall certainly address your queries, well may they all be resolved. तस्मात् ते अहं ब्रवीमि ॥

आत्मन एष प्राणो जायते । यथैषा पुरुषे छायैतस्मिन्नेतदाततं मनोकृतेनायात्यस्मिञ्छरीरे ॥ ३.३

ātmana eṣa prāṇo jāyate |  yathaiṣā puruṣe chāyaitasminnetadātataṃ manokṛtenāyātyasmiñcharīre ǁ 3.3

आत्मनः एषः प्राणः जायते । यथा एषा पुरुषे छाया एतस्मिन् एतत् आततं मनोकृतेन आयाति अस्मिन् शरीरे ॥

**3.3** This life energy is an offshoot of Brahman, the Shiva consciousness.पुरुषे छाया Prana is the silent shady envelope. It is the caressing, constantly comforting, undeniable aspect of God. एतस्मिन् आततं It is as if the power of God extended in creation. मनोकृतेन अस्मिन् शरीरे आयाति it is the link between mind and body. It is what ties a pure soul to the complex mind and yokes it to the body. It is as though a projection of the soul that desires to enjoy and experience. It is the reflection of life.

Prana links the mighty Sun's soul-rays to innumerable multifaceted dust particles, infusing each with godliness, making each alive.

छाया = Resemblance, **Reflection**, Shadow. Life is the Reflection of the Soul. Prana is the undeniable proof of Life. मनोकृतेन = Just as we know someone is Alive due to the movement of the Breath, similarly **by the working of his Mind** we know that he is unique, distinct, and separate from the rest.

मनोकृतेन = We have two interpretations of this powerful word. One interpretation is that the Brahman desires infinitely, and that leads to life, a composite of soul+mind+body all linked together by the breath. Brahman then plays its leela in various bodies, and after sometime it all resolves back. Then the cycle continues indefinitely…

# The Karmic Impression Driving Force

Another interpretation is that Brahman simply divides infinitely, and then each soul has a free-will that is _as if governed_ by the component called mind. Due to the mind's willing, the soul gets attached to specific bodies by the breath, enjoys for a while, then goes for a new body. After some cycles of enjoying in various bodies, it somehow gets the grace to align with the supreme. This is the theory of Karma.

यथा सम्राडेवाधिकृतान् विनियुङ्क्ते । एतान् ग्रामानेतान् ग्रामानधितिष्ठस्वेत्येवमेवैष प्राण इतरान् प्राणान् पृथक्पृथगेव सन्निधत्ते ॥ ३.४

yathā samrāḍevādhikṛtān viniyuṅkte | etān grāmānetān grāmānadhitiṣṭhasvetyevamevaiṣa prāṇa itarān prāṇān pṛthakpṛthageva sannidhatte ॥ 3.4

यथा सम्राट् एव अधिकृतान् विनियुङ्क्ते । एतान् ग्रामान् एतान् ग्रामान् अधितिष्ठस्व इति एवम् एव एषः प्राणः इतरान् प्राणान् पृथक् पृथक् एव सन्निधत्ते ॥

## Delegate and Relax

$3.4$ Just as a Father delegates responsibility to his progeny, यथा सम्राट् एव अधिकृतान् विनियुङ्क्ते

- just as a President divides the work according to the skills of his secretaries, एतान् ग्रामान् एतान् ग्रामान् अधितिष्ठस्व इति
- just as flowers bloom according to the seasons and tributaries branch out from the mighty Ganges,
- just as one fertilized egg gets differentiated into eyes, hands, heart or bone,

एवम् एव एषः प्राणः इतरान् प्राणान् पृथक् पृथक् एव सन्निधत्ते ॥

So does the life force split into various currents. Each current is wholly independent, responsible, and cut out for its work.

पायूपस्थेऽपानं चक्षुःश्रोत्रे मुखनासिकाभ्यां प्राणः स्वयं प्रातिष्ठते मध्ये तु समानः । एष ह्येतद्धुतमन्नं समं नयति तस्मादेताः सप्तार्चिषो भवन्ति ॥ ३.५

pāyūpasthe'pānaṃ cakṣuḥśrotre mukhanāsikābhyāṃ
prāṇaḥ svayaṃ prātiṣṭhate madhye tu samānaḥ |
eṣa hyetaddhutamannaṃ samaṃ nayati tasmādetāḥ
saptārciṣo bhavanti ∥ 3.5

पायु–उपस्थे अपानं चक्षुः–श्रोत्रे मुखनासिकाभ्यां प्राणः स्वयं प्रातिष्ठते मध्ये तु समानः । एषः हि एतत् हुतम् अन्नं समं नयति तस्मात् एताः सप्त अर्चिषः भवन्ति ॥

## Prana Apana Samana Vyana Udana
## Naga Kurma Devadatta Krikala Dhananjaya

The five Prana Vayu - Prana, Apana, Udana, Vyana and Samana.

The five Upaprana Vayu - Naga, Kurma, Devadatta, Krikala and Dhananjaya.

# 3.5

THROAT Vishuddhi Chakra-   Udana Vayu  Immunity
HEART   Anahata Chakra-      Prana Vayu Respiration
NAVEL   Manipura Chakra-     Samana Vayu Digestion
WHOLE  Swadisthana Chakra-Vyana Vayu Circulation
PELVIS  Mooladhara Chakra- Apana Vayu Evacuation

पायूपस्थे = In the पायुस् = organs of excretion, and in the उपस्थः = organs of pleasurable sex and reproduction; the energy current is named अपानं Apana. This Apana is a specific and distinct portion of the Life Force (Prana) that flows vertically downwards in the body. मुखनासिकाभ्यां = together with the mouth and nose in the region of the face consisting of the senses, the eyes, ears, etc., the energy current is named the same as स्वयम् itself viz. प्राणः Prana. This Prana is a specific and distinct portion of the Life Force (Prana) that flows vertically upwards in the body.

तस्मात् एताः सप्तार्चिषः भवन्ति ॥ The life force is thus split into 5 vayus for efficient governance. And it also gives rise to the 7 energy centers or chakras that regulate the being. सप्त seven अर्चिषः [m1/3] luminous flames *(from stem अर्चिष्)* I Chakras are luminous meaning functional, flames meaning powerful.

हृदि ह्येष आत्मा । अत्रैतदेकशतं नाडीनां तासां शतं शतमेकैकस्यां
द्वासप्ततिर्द्वासप्ततिः प्रतिशाखानाडीसहस्राणि भवन्त्यासु व्यानश्चरति ॥
३.६

hṛdi hyeṣa ātmā | atraitadekaśataṃ nāḍīnāṃ tāsāṃ śataṃ
śatamekaikasyāṃ dvāsaptatirdvāsaptatiḥ
pratiśākhānāḍīsahasrāṇi bhavantyāsu vyānaścarati || 3.6

हृदि हि एषः आत्मा । अत्र एतत् एकशतं नाडीनां तासां शतं शतम्
एक–एकस्यां द्वासप्ततिः द्वासप्ततिः प्रति–शाखा–नाडी–सहस्राणि
भवन्ति आसु व्यानः चरति ॥

## 72000 Nadis each in 100 of 101

3.6 एषः आत्मा हृदि वसति = The Soul is situated in the physical heart.

अत्र Here नाडीनाम् branching out of nerves. एतम् the एकशतम् 101 = From the heart region, 101 major tubular channels reach out to all parts of the Being.

तासाम् एकैकस्यां शतं शतं = Each of these 101 trunk lines contains a 100 branches.

प्रतिशाखानाडी सहस्राणि द्वासप्ततिः द्वासप्ततिः भवन्ति = Each of the 100 branches contains 72000 nadi, i.e. 101x100x72000=72,72,00,000=72crore & 72lakh nadi.

Sum Total of all large and medium and fine nadi = 101+10100+727200000 = 72,72,10,201.
72 crore 72 lakh 10 thousand 2 hundred and 1.

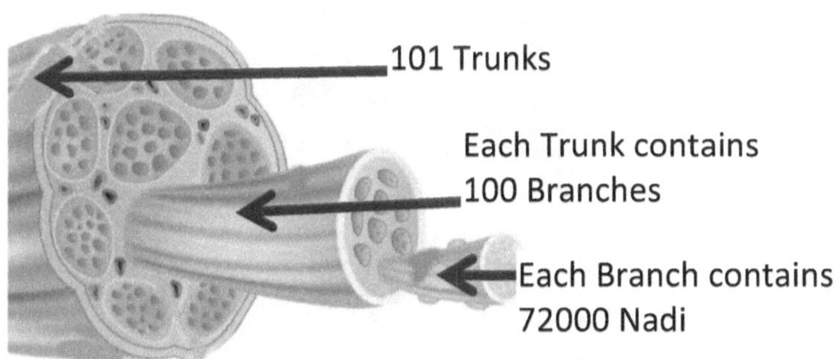


आसु $^{f7/3}$ व्यानः चरति ॥ Within these nadis, the Vyana Vayu moves. These are the arteries and veins of the circulatory system on the physical level. And the nerve pathways for the mind on the subtle level. And for the soul on the causal level.

Note – Some of these pathways may have only one function, others may have multiple. The identification and tagging of each nadi is done elsewhere in the Veda.

Pipal tree analogy. Heart is the Pipal Tree.
After a few years, many trunks grow out, consider that 101 trunks grow out.

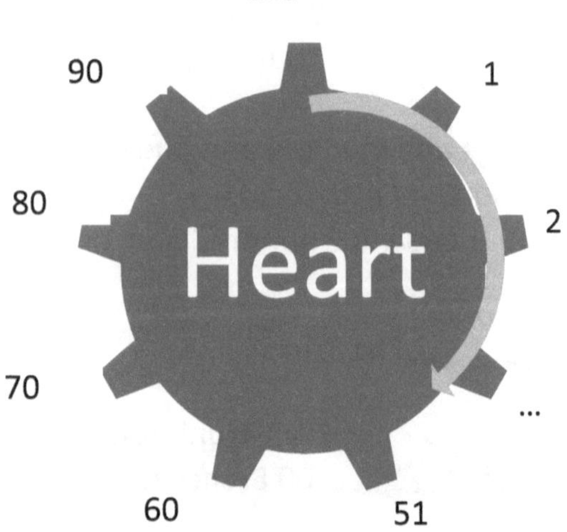



So now we have 101 trunks, and each trunk has 100 branches, as a thumb rule.

Of course, each branch will have many twigs and there are 72000 twigs in each branch.

Significance of 72000

72 = 1x72, 2x36, 3x24, 4x18, 6x12, 8x9.

- 36 is the number that represents all the Shaktis in creation, where the highest number 36 represents Shiva consciousness.
- 24 represents the Gayatri meter.
- 18 is the number that represents all the virtues of Devi.
- 12 is the number that represents all the constellations of the Zodiac, or possibilities for mind to be stabilized or distracted.
- 9 is the highest digit in the decimal system.
- 8 is the number that represents Infinity.

Since creation is a duality principle, 36x2 = 72. And the other numbers to allow for all possibilities for karmic theory to operate, and all probable paths to liberation.

अथैकयोर्ध्व उदानः पुण्येन पुण्यं लोकं नयति
पापेन पापमुभाभ्यामेव मनुष्यलोकम् ॥ ३.७

athaikayordhva udānaḥ puṇyena puṇyaṃ lokaṃ nayati
pāpena pāpamubhābhyāmeva manuṣyalokam ॥ 3.7

84

अथ एकया ऊर्ध्वः उदानः पुण्येन पुण्यं लोकं नयति
पापेन पापम् उभाभ्याम् एव मनुष्य–लोकम् ॥

$3.7$ अथ Now the उदानः Udana Vayu ऊर्ध्वः up and beyond नयति carries, (the soul with mind and memory and impressions and learning and leanings) the subtle and causal bodies.

एकया one who is by virtue pure and divine, for him the exit is by the Sushumna nadi, i.e. to merge in Brahman, from where there is no return, no further cycle of birth and death = no further cycle of hate, guilt, delusion, distraction.

पुण्येन पुण्यं लोकं = one who is by deeds the great, him to the world of celestial happiness = reborn as a star or celebrity = reborn as a rich and famous personality.

पापेन पापं = the unjust to the world of misery = reborn or fallen into abject poverty, illness and misfortune.

उभाभ्याम् एव मनुष्यलोकम् = the middling to the world of humans = reborn as an average individual with plans and struggle, delights and distraction.

आदित्यो ह वै बाह्यः प्राण उदयत्येष ह्येनं चाक्षुषं प्राणमनुगृह्णानः ।
पृथिव्यां या देवता सैषा पुरुषस्यापानमवष्टभ्यान्तरा यदाकाशः स
समानो वायुर्व्यानः ॥ ३.८

ādityo ha vai bāhyaḥ prāṇa udayatyeṣa hyenaṃ cākṣuṣaṃ prāṇamanugṛhṇānaḥ | pṛthivyāṃ yā devatā saiṣā puruṣasyāpānamavaṣṭabhyāntarā yadākāśaḥ sa samāno vāyurvyānaḥ || 3.8

आदित्यः ह वै बाह्यः प्राणः उदयति एषः हि एनं चाक्षुषं प्राणम्
अनुगृह्णानः । पृथिव्यां या देवता सा एषा पुरुषस्य अपानम् अवष्टभ्य
अन्तरा यत् आकाशः सः समानः वायुः व्यानः ॥

# Light Earth Space Air

$3.8$ A verse that explains the functioning of the cosmos w.r.t. the five prana vayu studied earlier.

आदित्यः ह वै बाह्यः प्राणः उदयति एषः हि एनं चाक्षुषं प्राणम् अनुगृह्णानः

Prana Vayu in its external nature is equated to the Sun and sunlight, as it energizes the eyes and bestows sight to all.

पृथिव्यां या देवता सा एषा पुरुषस्य अपानम् अवष्टभ्य

Apana Vayu in its external nature is equated to the Earth goddess, the strong loving gravitational pull that keeps us firmly anchored.

अन्तरा यत् आकाशः सः समानः

Samana Vayu in its external nature is equated to the vast Space, with billions of stars, galaxies, clusters, and cosmic dust.

वायुः व्यानः ॥

Vyana Vayu in its external nature is equated to Air and atmosphere, that which keeps the heart pumping, keeps all bodies alive.

---

As microcosm so the macrocosm यत् पिण्डे तत् ब्रह्माण्डे ।

तेजो ह वा उदानस्तस्मादुपशान्ततेजाः ।
पुनर्भवमिन्द्रियैर्मनसि सम्पद्यमानैः ॥ ३.९

tejo ha vā udānastasmādupaśāntatejāḥ |

punarbhavamindriyairmanasi sampadyamānaiḥ || 3.9

तेजः ह वै उदानः तस्मात् उपशान्ततेजाः ।
पुनर्भवम् इन्द्रियैः मनसि सम्पद्य-मानैः ॥

## Water

**3.9** What carries the soul? Don't we say Water is Amrita, the Nectar. Doesn't a parched land give infinite blessings when the rain falls? Doesn't milk gratify the soul of each being?

Udana Vayu in its external nature is equated to $H_2O$, that which restores man, tree, flower or machine.

Note – तेज: Tejas in other contexts is also translated as Life, luster, or Fire. In this context its meaning "Life" is apt. This completes the discussion on the five elements that compose as well as govern creation. Since 4 elements have already been said, the 5th is water.

Further, उपशान्ततेजाः , when the waters have run dry, life diminishes and ebbs away. As evident in deserts that teem with oases during the monsoons, and become empty lands during other times.

मनसि सम्पद्यमानैः इन्द्रियैः Mind bundled together with the senses, baggage packed with the emotions, impressions, and learning,

पुनर्भवं प्रतिपद्यन्ते life departs from this body, and after a while, elsewhere, it springs anew.

This is commonplace as evident in the migratory birds, salmon fishes, corals, and hunters.

यच्चित्तस्तेनैष प्राणमायाति प्राणस्तेजसा युक्तः ।
सहात्मना यथासङ्कल्पितं लोकं नयति ॥ ३.१०

yaccittastenaiṣa prāṇamāyāti prāṇastejasā yuktaḥ |
sahātmanā yathāsaṅkalpitaṃ lokaṃ nayati ॥ 3.10

यत् चित्तः तेन एषः प्राणम् आयाति प्राणः तेजसा युक्तः ।
सह आत्मना यथा सङ्कल्पितं लोकं नयति ॥

एषः यत् चितः भवति This which in_the_thought is (at the hour of death, that strong desire is bundled and) led by the Prana.

प्राणः तेजसा युक्तः सन् Prana (= Life force) with_the_Tejas (= Udana Vayu) being united,

आत्मना सह and with the Soul (inner being)

यथा संकल्पितं as strongly wished (in the end moment)

लोकम् नयति to (an another) world carries.

# Final Thought Rules

**3.10** This verse is a Maha Vakya. It is a Supreme statement. It states an inviolable truth.

At the hour of Death, the Thought predominant in the mind becomes the Basis for the new birth, i.e. governs the parameters like place of birth, parents, resources, happiness and further evolution.

This is easily verified by observing and noting down the last thought at bedtime. First thought in the morning while getting up shall be the same.

Another example is that we might be thinking, "Shall I go to Bombay or shall I go to Ambernath? Shall I wear this dress or that"? In the end where I go and what I wear is determined by the final thought. This is so evident is everyday life in all matters and in all decisions.

य एवं विद्धान् प्राणं वेद । न हास्य प्रजा हीयतेऽमृतो भवति तदेषः श्लोकः ॥ ३.११

ya evaṃ vidvān prāṇaṃ veda | na hāsya prajā hīyate'mṛto bhavati tadeṣaḥ ślokaḥ || 3.11

यः एवं विद्धान् प्राणं वेद । न ह अस्य प्रजाः हीयते अमृतः भवति तत् एषः श्लोकः ॥

## Benefits of Upanishad

3.11 यः विद्वान् एवं प्राणं वेद the mature one who thus understands the working of the Prana,

अस्य प्रजाः न ह हीयते his progeny, family, village and neighborhood never comes to ruin, knows no grief,

सः अमृतः भवति he becomes immortal, he is revered and his life becomes the ideal for countless generations.

तत् एषः श्लोकः ॥ that is the essence of this verse which is also elucidated in the next verse.

This summarizes the benefits of understanding life in a bigger context and leading a visionary life accordingly. This is the Upanishad in practice.

उत्पत्तिमायर्ति स्थानं विभुत्वं चैव पञ्चधा ।
अध्यात्मं चैव प्राणस्य विज्ञायामृतमश्नुते विज्ञायामृतमश्नुत इति ॥३.१२

utpattimāyatim sthānam vibhutvam caiva pañcadhā |
adhyātmam caiva prāṇasya vijñāyāmṛtamaśnute
vijñāyāmṛtamaśnuta iti ॥  3.12

उत्पत्तिम् आयर्ति स्थानं विभुत्वं च एव पञ्चधा ।
अध्यात्मं च एव प्राणस्य विज्ञाय अमृतम् अश्नुते विज्ञाय अमृतम् अश्नुते इति ॥

# Learn Sudarshan Kriya=Master the Breath

3.12 प्राज्ञः प्राणस्य In-depth knowledge of the Breath.

उत्पत्तिम् Its origin, आयर्ति the inhalation and exhalation speed, depth, and timing, स्थानं the placement and importance of the 7 chakras

बिभुत्वं च एव पञ्चधा and its relation and functioning in the 5 major systems (respiration, excretion, digestion, circulation, immunity vis-a-vis endocrine)

च एव अध्यात्मं विज्ञाय and thus having known one's soul, what it is and what it takes to reveal it,

अमृतम् अश्नुते a human attains immortality. Reaches over to the plane of happiness. Crosses the dangerous self-defeating waters. Rises above hatred, suspicion, guilt, and bitterness. Becomes freed from self-imposed prison.
"विज्ञाय अमृतम् अश्नुते again repeated" to give force to this statement. To give surety.

इति ॥ Full Stop. End of this teaching. End of this term. End of this class. Break for now.

95

# 4<sup>th</sup> Question by Garg

## What is Sleep? What is Dream?

Very well explained here.


## Sleeping Awake Dreaming Comfort

अथ हैनं सौर्यायणी गार्ग्यः पप्रच्छ । भगवन्नेतस्मिन् पुरुषे कानि
स्वपन्ति कान्यस्मिञ्जाग्रति कतर एष देवः स्वप्नान् पश्यति कस्यैतत्सुखं
भवति कस्मिन्नु सर्वे सम्प्रतिष्ठिता भवन्तीति ॥ ४.१

atha hainaṃ sauryāyaṇī gārgyaḥ papraccha |
bhagavannetasmin puruṣe kāni svapanti kānyasmiñjāgrati
katara eṣa devaḥ svapnān paśyati kasyaitatsukhaṃ bhavati
kasminnu sarve sampratiṣṭhitā bhavantīti ॥  4.1

अथ ह एनं सौर्यायणी गार्ग्यः पप्रच्छ । भगवन् एतस्मिन् पुरुषे कानि
स्वपन्ति कानि अस्मिन् जाग्रति कतरे एषः देवः स्वप्नान् पश्यति कस्य
एतत् सुखं भवति कस्मिन् उ सर्वे सम्प्रतिष्ठिताः भवन्तीति ॥


एतस्मिन् m7/1 एतद् , अस्मिन् m7/1 इदम्

तद् एतद् इदम् अदस् Four distinct words. All mean "it".
However in Vedic usage, there is an added sense of the
relative separation from "it". The distance is not really
physical. The separation is an emotional distance or the
distance for one's thought to travel. As an analogy,
consider the separation of one's dress, one's skin, one's
heart and one's ego from the Soul. To quantify these
distances, Vedic terminology uses

- तद् for dress
- एतद् for skin
- इदम् for heart
- अदस् for ego

**4.1** अथ Now सौर्यायणी the Grandson of Surya the sun-god, गार्ग्यः of the dynasty of Garg = Gārgya, पप्रच्छ specially asked. एनं this:

भगवन् O Lord! एतस्मिन् पुरुषे कानि स्वपन्ति Inside this being who all sleep?

अस्मिन् कानि जाग्रति Within who are awake?

कतरः एषः देवः स्वप्नान् पश्यति Which of the two beings sees dreams? (Whether the one that sleeps or the one that is awake).

कस्य Of whose एतत् this सुखं pleasure and comfort भवति is?

कस्मिन् In what सर्वे all humans संप्रतिष्ठिताः well established भवन्ति are?

तस्मै स होवाच । यथा गार्ग्य मरीचयोऽर्कस्यास्तं गच्छतः सर्वा एतस्मिंस्तेजोमण्डल एकीभवन्ति । ताः पुनः पुनरुदयतः प्रचरन्त्येवं ह वै तत्सर्वं परे देवे मनस्येकीभवति । तेन तर्ह्येष पुरुषो न श्रृणोति न पश्यति न जिघ्रति न रसयते न स्पृशते नाभिवदते नादत्ते नानन्दयते न विसृजते नेयायते स्वपितीत्याचक्षते ॥ ४.२

tasmai sa hovāca | yathā gārgya marīcayo'rkasyāstam gacchataḥ sarvā etasmiṃstejomaṇḍala ekībhavanti | tāḥ punaḥ punarudayataḥ pracarantyevaṃ ha vai tatsarvaṃ pare deve manasyekībhavati | tena tarhyeṣa puruṣo na śṛṇoti na paśyati na jighrati na rasayate na spṛśate nābhivadate nādatte nānandayate na visṛjate neyāyate svapitītyācakṣate || 4.2


तस्मै सः ह उवाच । यथा गार्ग्य मरीचयः अर्कस्य अस्तं गच्छतः सर्वाः एतस्मिन् तेजोमण्डले एकी–भवन्ति । ताः पुनः पुनः उदयतः प्रचरन्ति एवं ह वै तत् सर्वं परे देवे मनसि एकी–भवति । तेन तर्हि एषः पुरुषः न श्रृणोति न पश्यति न जिघ्रति न रसयते न स्पृशते न अभिवदते न आदत्ते न आनन्दयते न विसृजते न इयायते स्वपिति इति आचक्षते ॥

## Deep Sleep State

4.2 सः तस्मै उवाच He to him replied. (The Master answered the disciple).

गार्ग्य O Garg! यथा अस्तं गच्छतः अर्कस्य Just as in the setting of the Sun,
सर्वाः मरीचयः all the sunrays एतस्मिन् तेजोमण्डले of this fiery orb एकीभवन्ति become withdrawn,
पुनः उद्यतः अर्कस्य and again with the rising of the sun
ताः पुनः प्रचरन्ति they once more shine forth,

एवं ह तत् सर्वं Similarly all folk परे देवे एकीभवति in the supreme being become resolved मनसि it is the mind that shuts down, it is the mental faculties that come to a standstill in the Brahman. (Just as our thoughts slowdown in the presence of the Master, just as we are left speechless, thoughtless in Guruji's presence).

तेन तर्हि एषः पुरुषः Indeed the state in which a person

न श्रुणोति hears not न पश्यति sees not न जिघ्रति smells not न रसयते tastes not न स्पृशते touches not न अभिवदते speaks not even a little न आदत्ते eats not न आनन्दयते displays excitement not न विसृजते evacuates not न इयायते roams not

तदा स्वपिति then he sleeps;
इति आचक्षते thus the wise say.

प्राणाग्नय एवैतस्मिन् पुरे जाग्रति । गार्हपत्यो ह वा एषोऽपानो व्यानोऽन्वाहार्यपचनो यद् गार्हपत्यात् प्रणीयते प्रणयनादाहवनीयः प्राणः ॥ ४.३

pranāgnaya evaitasmin pure jāgrati | gārhapatyo ha vā eṣo'pāno vyāno'nvāhāryapacano yad gārhapatyāt praṇīyate praṇayanādāhavanīyaḥ prāṇaḥ ॥ 4.3

प्राण–अग्नयः एव एतस्मिन् पुरे जाग्रति । गार्हपत्यः ह वै एषः अपानः व्यानः अन्वाहार्य–पचनः यत् गार्हपत्यात् प्रणीयते प्रणयनात् आहवनीयः प्राणः ॥

Tretagni = Garhapatya-Dakshinagni-Ahavaniya

## 4.3 During deep sleep state;

एतस्मिन् पुरे Inside this city (body-mind complex of the person)
प्राणाग्नयः एव जाग्रति the currents of Prana alone are awake, up and about.
एषः अपानः वै गार्हपत्यः this Apana Vayu is verily the housemaid, cleaning away all the leftover thoughts and emotions;
व्यानः अन्वाहार्यपचनः the Vyana Vayu is verily the incessant circulation, doing its task meticulously;
यत् गार्हपत्यात् प्रणयनात् प्रणीयते Which from the cleaned mind (due to Apana Vayu) breathes,
प्राणः एव आहवनीयः that Prana Vayu now respires cheerfully, restoring the mind's confidence and vision.

During a Yagya, a large Homa spread over several days, e.g. the Navaratri or Somayagya, three homa kunds are especially made to honor the Vayus. These are accordingly named गार्हपत्यः (Garhapatya Agni) to honor Apana Vayu, अन्वाहार्यपचनः (Dakshin Agni) to honor Vyana Vayu, and आहवनीयः (Ahavaniya Agni) to honor Prana Vayu.

Honoring is the key in festivals and celebrations. Honoring leads to all round bliss, growth and success.

यदुच्छ्वासनिःश्वासावेतावाहुती समं नयतीति स समानः । मनो ह वाव यजमानः । इष्टफलमेवोदानः । स एनं यजमानमहरहर्ब्रह्म गमयति ॥ ४.४

yaducchvāsaniḥśvāsāvetāvāhutī samaṃ nayatīti sa samānaḥ | mano ha vāva yajamānaḥ |

iṣṭaphalamevodānaḥ | sa enaṃ

yajamānamaharaharbrahma gamayati || 4.4

यत् उच्छ्वास–निःश्वासौ एतौ आहुती समं नयति इति सः समानः । मनः ह वाव यजमानः । इष्टफलम् एव उदानः । सः एनं यजमानम् अहरहः ब्रह्म गमयति ॥

4.4 यत् एतौ उच्छ्वासन- निश्वासन Just as exhalation and inhalation are both आहुती needed समं नयति to maintain proper balance, इति सः समानः so is the functioning of Samana Vayu that digests equitably as needed; in this respect the Samana Vayu is like होता the officiating chief priest in a Yagya who directs each offering properly.

Note – Since Homa, Fire Ritual, Yagya are the events that bind a family together, maintain unity and harmony in a village, so the Upanishad uses it as an analogy to highlight and explain in detail the functioning of the breath. This level of detail for the breath is given so that Man can implement Pranayama in daily life. The power of breath is repeatedly told; it is to bring man's focus and attention to learn Yogic breathing techniques (like the Sudarshan Kriya in the 21$^{st}$ century).

मनः ह यजमानः उदानः एव the mind is verily balanced by the Udana Vayu that provides immunity, just as the Organizer of a Yagya gets the credit for ensuring safety in society.

इष्टफलं सः एनं यजमानं He delivers the chosen fruit to (the organizer) this organized body-mind complex, अहरहः day by day eventually ब्रह्म गमयति leads man towards liberation.

Man might take a few life-times to attain Nirvana. Each exit of man from one body to another is enforced by the Udana Vayu. The Udana Vayu safely transports the soul along with the mind in its current state of evolution, each time, in each birth.

अत्रैष देवः स्वप्ने महिमानमनुभवति । यद् दृष्टं दृष्टमनुपश्यति श्रुतं
श्रुतमेवार्थमनुशृणोति देशदिगन्तरैश्च प्रत्यनुभूतं पुनः पुनः प्रत्यनुभवति
दृष्टं चादृष्टं च श्रुतं चाश्रुतं चानुभूतं चाननुभूतं च सच्चासच्च सर्वं पश्यति
सर्वः पश्यति ॥ ४.५

atraiṣa devaḥ svapne mahimānamanubhavati |
yad dṛṣṭaṃ dṛṣṭamanupaśyati śrutaṃ
śrutamevārthamanuśṛṇoti deśadigantaraiśca
pratyanubhūtaṃ punaḥ punaḥ pratyanubhavati dṛṣṭaṃ
cādṛṣṭaṃ ca śrutaṃ cāśrutaṃ cānubhūtaṃ cānanubhūtaṃ
ca saccāsacca sarvaṃ paśyati sarvaḥ paśyati ॥  4.5

अत्र एषः देवः स्वप्ने महिमानम् अनुभवति । यत् दृष्टं दृष्टम् अनुपश्यति
श्रुतं श्रुतम् एव अर्थम् अनुशृणोति देश–दिक्–अन्तरैः च प्रति–अनुभूतं
पुनः पुनः प्रति–अनुभवति दृष्टं च अदृष्टं च श्रुतं च अश्रुतं च अनुभूतं च
अन्–अनुभूतं च सत् च असत् च सर्वं पश्यति सर्वः पश्यति ॥

## Dream State

4.5 एषः देवः this human being अत्र स्वप्ने while in the dream state महिमानं glory and grandeur अनुभवति experiences.

यत् दृष्टं दृष्टं अनुपश्यति whichever sights and scenes man hath previously seen he conjures to see,

श्रुतं श्रुतम् एव अर्थम् अनुश्रृणोति whatever sounds and noises man hath previously heard he conjures to hear,

देशादिगन्तरैः च and in various lands प्रत्यनुभूतं whatever his senses sought and his reasoning established, पुनः पुनः again and again in varying fashion प्रत्यनुभवति he replays those moments up close in dreams.

दृष्टं च अदृष्टं seen and never seen before श्रुतम् अश्रुतं heard and never heard before अनुभूतं अननुभूतं च experienced and never experienced सत् असत् real and unreal सर्वं पश्यति all such events he sees fancifully in the dreams.

स्वयमपि सन् सर्वः पश्यति the doer, the lead actor himself becoming, all dreams he enjoys.

स यदा तेजसाऽभिभूतो भवति । अत्रैष देवः स्वप्नान् न पश्यत्यथ
यदैतस्मिञ्छरीरे एतत्सुखं भवति ॥ ४.६

sa yadā tejasā'bhibhūto bhavati | atraiṣa devaḥ svapnān

na paśyatyatha yadaitasmiñcharīre etatsukhaṃ bhavati ||
4.6

सः यदा तेजसा अभिभूतः भवति । अत्र एषः देवः स्वप्नान् न पश्यति
अथ यत् एतस्मिन् शरीरे एतत् सुखं भवति ॥

---

स यथा सोम्य वयांसि वसोवृक्षं सम्प्रतिष्ठन्ते एवं ह वै तत्सर्वं पर
आत्मनि सम्प्रतिष्ठते ॥ ४.७

sa yathā sobhya vayāṃsi vasovṛkṣaṃ sampratiṣṭhante
evaṃ ha vai tatsarvaṃ para ātmani sampratiṣṭhate || 4.7

सः यथा सोम्य वयांसि वसो–वृक्षं सम्प्रतिष्ठन्ते एवं ह वै तत् सर्वं परे
आत्मनि सम्प्रतिष्ठते ॥

## Comfort State

**4.6** In the flash of a moment, the dream shuts off, and the human being in this body feels comforted. Experiences pleasurable bliss. A state of restful joy pervades his being.

**4.7** हे सौम्य O dear child! यथा वयांसि Just as birds वासोवृक्षं सम्प्रतिष्ठन्ते retire to their chosen tree for the night,

एवं ह तत् सर्वं परं आत्मनि सम्प्रतिष्ठते similarly, a time comes when all beings fall in the state of deep sleep, they disconnect from the mind and senses and memories, and they experience deep rest.

Note – The Upanishad is simply expressing a forgotten fact. Each one of us, whether mighty or forlorn, whether bird or bee, plant or animal, each and every being at one point or another experiences the state of comforting rest.

For the saint this is a common thing, for animals and plants also it is quite commonplace. Only for mankind it seems to be forgotten, rare, and elusive. Still it happens.

The state of non-anxiety, the state of calmness, this pristine state of non-doership has been bestowed on all beings in creation.

पृथिवी च पृथिवीमात्रा चापश्चापोमात्रा च तेजश्च तेजोमात्रा च वायुश्च वायुमात्रा चाकाशश्चाकाशामात्रा च चक्षुश्च द्रष्टव्यं च श्रोत्रं च श्रोतव्यं च घ्राणं च घ्रातव्यं च रसश्च रसयितव्यं च त्वक्च स्पर्शयितव्यं च वाक्च वक्तव्यं च हस्तौ चादातव्यं चोपस्थश्चानन्दयितव्यं च पायुश्च विसर्जयितव्यं च पादौ च गन्तव्यं च मनश्च मन्तव्यं च बुद्धिश्च बोद्धव्यं चाहङ्कारश्चाहङ्कर्तव्यं च चित्तं च चेतयितव्यं च तेजश्च विद्योतयितव्यं च प्राणश्च विद्यारयितव्यं च ॥ ४.८

prthivī ca pṛthivīmātrā cāpaścāpomātrā ca tejaśca
tejomātrā ca vāyuśca vāyumātrā cākāśaścākāśamātrā ca
cakṣuśca draṣṭavyaṃ ca śrotraṃ ca śrotavyaṃ ca ghrāṇaṃ
ca ghrātavyaṃ ca rasaśca rasayitavyaṃ ca tvakca
sparśayitavyaṃ ca vākca vaktavyaṃ ca hastau cādātavyaṃ
copasthaścānandayitavyaṃ ca pāyuśca visarjayitavyaṃ ca
pādau ca gantavyaṃ ca manaśca mantavyaṃ ca buddhiśca
boddhavyaṃ cāhaṅkāraścāhaṅkartavyaṃ ca cittaṃ ca
cetayitavyaṃ ca tejaśca vidyotayitavyaṃ ca prāṇaśca
vidyārayitavyaṃ ca ॥  4.8


पृथिवी च पृथिवी–मात्रा च आपः च आपो–मात्रा च तेजः च तेजो–मात्रा च वायुः च वायु–मात्रा च आकाशः च आकाश–मात्रा च चक्षुः च द्रष्टव्यं च श्रोत्रं च श्रोतव्यं च घ्राणं च घ्रातव्यं च रसश्च रसयितव्यं च त्वक्च स्पर्शयितव्यं च वाक्च वक्तव्यं च हस्तौ चा आदातव्यं च उपस्थः च आनन्दयितव्यं च पायुः च विसर्जयितव्यं च पादौ च गन्तव्यं च मनः च मन्तव्यं च बुद्धिः च बोद्धव्यं च अहङ्कारः च अहङ्कर्तव्यं च चित्तं च चेतयितव्यं च तेजः च विद्योतयितव्यं च प्राणः च विद्यारयितव्यं च ॥

# Physical Elements & Subtle Counterparts

4.8 पृथिवी पृथिवीमात्रा च the solid earth and the subtle earth element that is present in everything including the mind,

आपः आपोमात्रा च the flowing waters and the subtle water element that is present in everything including the mind,

तेजः च तेजोमात्रा च the physical fire and the subtle fire element that is present in everything including the mind,

वायुः च वायुमात्रा च the effervescent air and the subtle air element that is present in everything including the mind,

आकाशः च आकाशमात्रा च the vast space and the subtle space element that is present in everything including the mind,

चक्षुः च द्रष्टव्यं च the beautiful eyes and the visible objects and the act of seeing that is a faculty of the mind,

श्रोत्रं च श्रोतव्यं च the physical ears and the heard sounds and the act of hearing that is a faculty of the mind,

घ्राणं च घ्रातव्यं च the pesky nose and the inhaled fragrances and the act of smelling that is a faculty of the mind,

रसः च रसयितव्यं च the smooth tongue and the tasty delicacies and the act of tasting that is a faculty of the mind,

त्वक् च स्पर्शयितव्यं च the tender skin and the contacted beings and the act of touching that is a faculty of the mind,

वाक् च वक्तव्यं च the sharp tongue and the elaborate speeches and the act of speaking that is willed by the mind,

हस्तौ च आदातव्यं च the firm hands and the grasped gadgets and the act of grasping that is willed by the mind,

उपस्थः च आनन्दयितव्यं च the conjugal organ and the pleasure giving partner and the act of making love that is willed by the mind,

पायुः च विसर्जयितव्यं च the evacuating organs and the evacuee and the act of evacuation that is willed by the mind,

पादौ च गन्तव्यम् the sturdy feet and the swift movements and the act of travelling that is willed by the mind,

मनः च मन्तव्यं च the sensing mind and the sensed thoughts and the act of thinking that is willed by the self,

बुद्धिः च बोधव्यं च the sane intellect and the pragmatic decision making and the act of reasoning that is willed by the self,

अहङ्कारः च अहङ्कर्तव्यम् च the impartial ego and the discriminations and the act of mineness that is willed by the self,

चित्तं च चेतयितव्यं च the full memory and the storehouse of emotions and the act of remembering that is willed by the self,

तेजः विद्योतयितव्यं च the essential wisdom and the known and the act of knowing that is willed by the self,

प्राणः च विधारयितव्यं च the life and the living and the act of sustenance that is willed by the self.

एष हि द्रष्टा स्रष्टा श्रोता घ्राता रसयिता मन्ता बोद्धा कर्ता विज्ञानात्मा पुरुषः । स परेऽक्षर आत्मनि सम्प्रतिष्ठते ॥ ४.९

eṣa hi draṣṭā spraṣṭā śrotā ghrātā rasayitā mantā boddhā kartā vijñānātmā puruṣaḥ | sa pare'kṣara ātmani sampratiṣṭhate || 4.9

एषः हि द्रष्टा स्रष्टा श्रोता घ्राता रसयिता मन्ता बोद्धा कर्ता विज्ञान– आत्मा पुरुषः । सः परे अक्षरे आत्मनि सम्प्रतिष्ठते ॥

परमेवाक्षरं प्रतिपद्यते स यो ह वै तदच्छायमशरीरमलोहितं शुभ्रमक्षरं वेदयते यस्तु सोम्य । स सर्वज्ञः सर्वो भवति । तदेष श्लोकः ॥ ४.१०

paramevākṣaraṃ pratipadyate sa yo ha vai tadacchāyamaśarīramalohitaṃ śubhramakṣaraṃ vedayate yastu somya |  sa sarvajñaḥ sarvo bhavati |  tadeṣa ślokaḥ || 4.10

परम् एव अक्षरं प्रतिपद्यते सः यः ह वै तत् अच्छायम् अशरीरम् अलोहितं शुभ्रम् अक्षरं वेदयते यस्तु सोम्य । सः सर्वज्ञः सर्वः भवति । तत् एषः श्लोकः ॥

# Individual Soul - Collective Consciousness

4.9 एषः हि Verily he द्रष्टा the Seer स्रष्टा the Experiencer श्रोता the Listener घ्राता the Smeller रसयिता the Taster मन्ता the thought bundle बोद्धा the Judge कर्ता the Doer विज्ञानात्मा the intelligent Soul पुरुषः the Being,

सः परे अक्षरे आत्मनि सम्प्रतिष्ठते He; in the beyond, in the eternal, in the Supreme Consciousness, is well absorbed-perfectly merged.

---

4.10 यः ह वै Verily that person who तत् This अव्ययं undifferentiated अशरीरं unembodied अलोहितम् unbiased शुभ्रम् brilliant अक्षरं imperishable (soul) वेदयते recognizes,

सः परम् अक्षरम् एव प्रतिपद्यते । That person with the unfathomable eternal soul attains oneness.

सौम्य O dear one! यः तु एवं विद्वान् definitely the one who likewise understands (this teaching) सः सर्वज्ञः सर्वः भवति he becomes omniscient, he becomes omnipresent.

तत् एषः श्लोकः भवति THAT, this verse summarizes, and it is also elucidated in the next verse.

विज्ञानात्मा सह देवैश्च सर्वैः प्राणा भूतानि सम्प्रतिष्ठन्ति यत्र ।
तदक्षरं वेदयते यस्तु सोम्य स सर्वज्ञः सर्वमेवाविवेशेति ॥ ४.११

vijñānātmā saha devaiśca sarvaiḥ prāṇā bhūtāni
sampratiṣṭhanti yatra |
tadakṣaraṃ vedayate yastu somya sa sarvajñaḥ
sarvamevāviveśeti ‖  4.11


विज्ञान–आत्मा सह देवैः च सर्वैः प्राणाः भूतानि सम्प्रतिष्ठन्ति यत्र ।
तत् अक्षरं वेदयते यस्तु सोम्य सः सर्वज्ञः सर्वम् एव आविवेश इति ॥

**4.11** यत्र Wherein सर्वैः देवैः सह all beings endowed with प्राणाः the Prana Vayus and भूतानि the five elements सम्प्रतिष्ठन्ति are well contained,

सौम्य O gentle boy! तु certainly विज्ञानात्मा the wise man यः who तत् THAT अक्षरं imperishable soul वेदयते glimpses,

सः He सर्वज्ञः the omniscient one सर्वम् एव आविवेश is hailed as the one who has permeated the entire creation.

इति full stop. End of the class. End of this teaching.

# 5<sup>th</sup> Question by Satyakama

## How is the primal sound OM relevant?

Very well explained here.

अथ हैनं शैब्यः सत्यकामः पप्रच्छ । स यो ह वै तद् भगवन् मनुष्येषु प्रायणान्तमोङ्कारमभिध्यायीत । कतमं वाव स तेन लोकं जयतीति तस्मै स होवाच ॥ ५.१

atha hainaṃ śaibyaḥ satyakāmaḥ papraccha |
sa yo ha vai tad bhagavan manuṣyeṣu
prāyaṇāntamoṅkāramabhidhyāyīta | katamaṃ vāva sa
tena lokaṃ jayatīti tasmai sa hovāca ॥ 5.1


अथ ह एनं शैब्यः सत्यकामः पप्रच्छ । सः यो ह वै भगवन् मनुष्येषु प्रायणान्तं ॐकारम् अभिध्यायीत । कतमं वै इव सः तेन लोकं जयति इति तस्मै सः ह उवाच ॥


एतद् वै सत्यकाम परं चापरं च ब्रह्म यदोङ्कारः । तस्माद् विद्वान् एतेनैवाऽऽयतनेनैकतरमन्वेति ॥ ५.२

etad vai satyakāma paraṃ cāparaṃ ca brahma yadoṅkāraḥ
| tasmād vidvān etenaivā''yatanenaikataramanveti ॥ 5.2


एतत् वै सत्यकाम परं च अपरं च ब्रह्म यत् ॐकारः । तस्मात् विद्वान् एतेन एव आयतनेन एकतरम् अन्वेति ॥

**5.1** अथ In due sequence then सत्यकामः Satyakama the righteous, शैब्यः the son of Shibi, पप्रच्छ devotedly enquired regarding एनं this topic:

भगवन् O All Knowing One! मनुष्येषु Amongst all humans सः he यः who प्रायणान्तं regularly till his last breath, तत् THAT ॐकारम् OM the Primal Sound अभिध्यायीत earnestly and properly chants and meditates upon,

सः he कतमं to which लोकं meritorious plane जयति attains?

इति । This is all I wish to know, nothing else.

तस्मै To him (Satyakama) सः he (the master Pippalada) उवाच replied ह gladdened.

---

**5.2** सत्यकाम O Righteous One! यत् ॐकारः O what of OM! The luxurious, the abundant, the all fulfilling divine…
एतत् THIS वै certainly is परं ब्रह्म the transcendental Brahman च and अपरं the worldly great च as well.
तस्मात् Hence विद्वान् a sincere practitioner,
एतेन by its आयतनेन help एकतरम् one of the two (wonderful planes) अन्वेति wins.

स यद्येकमात्रमभिध्यायीत स तेनैव संवेदितस्तूर्णमेव जगत्यामभिसम्पद्यते । तमृचो मनुष्यलोकमुपनयन्ते स तत्र तपसा ब्रह्मचर्येण श्रद्धया सम्पन्नो महिमानमनुभवति ॥ ५.३

sa yadyekamātramabhidhyāyīta sa tenaiva saṃveditastūrṇameva jagatyāmabhisampadyate | tamṛco manuṣyalokamupanayante sa tatra tapasā brahmacaryeṇa śraddhayā sampanno mahimānamanubhavati ॥ 5.3

सः यदि एकमात्रम् अभिध्यायीत सः तेन एव संवेदितः तूर्णम् एव जगत्याम् अभिसम्पद्यत्ते । तं ऋचः मनुष्यलोकम् उपनयन्ते सः तत्र तपसा ब्रह्मचर्येण श्रद्धया सम्पन्नः महिमानम् अनुभवति ॥

# OM - its first matra अम्

**5.3** यदि if सः he एकमात्रम् the first matra अभिध्यायीत earnestly practices and meditates upon,

सः he तेन by it एव surely संवेदितः realizes a most wonderful thing. तूर्णम् Quickly एव it is guaranteed जगत्याम् in this world अभिसम्पद्यत्ते he attains a high and wealthy position due to his earnest endeavor.

ऋचः The sacred hymns describing the inviolable cosmic laws उपनयन्ते propel तं him मनुष्यलोकम् to the elite class.

तत्र There सः he तपसा by hard-work ब्रह्मचर्येण by balanced lifestyle श्रद्धया by faith and trust सम्पन्नः luxurious महिमानम् living अनुभवति realizes.

Very quickly, the person achieves a big status. It is guaranteed that greatness will come to him.

By meditating on the first matra अम् with attention on the Manipura Chakra, the cosmic laws get revealed as described in the Rigveda. The theoretical mind becomes sharp. Mathematical concepts become well understood. Thereby a person's talents shine and he attains to wealth and fame in the world of men.

He adheres to the laws and customs of good citizenship, this is the reason his talents propel him to the elite class in society.

अथ यदि द्विमात्रेण मनसि सम्पद्यते सोऽन्तरिक्षं यजुर्भिरुन्नीयते सोमलोकम् । स सोमलोके विभूतिमनुभूय पुनरावर्तते ॥ ५.४

atha yadi dvimātreṇa manasi sampadyate so'ntarikṣaṃ yajurbhirunnīyate somalokam | sa somaloke vibhūtimanubhūya punarāvartate || 5.4

अथ यदि द्विमात्रेण मनसि सम्पद्यते सः अन्तरिक्षं यजुर्भिः उन्नीयते सोमलोकम् । सः सोमलोके विभूतिम् अनुभुय पुनः आवर्तते ॥

अथ However,

यदि द्विमात्रेण अभिध्यायीत if a person would practice meditation on the first and second matra of OM,

तदा मनसि सम्पद्यते then in the mind a wondrous blossoming occurs.

यजुर्भिः By the hymns of the Yajurveda सः he अन्तरिक्षं to the solar system सोमलोकम् consisting of the moon and planets उन्नीयते rises to.

सोमलोके In the solar system सः he अनुभुय having attained विभूतिम् to fame पुनः again आवर्तते returns to earth since he maintains attachment to worldly plane.

# OM - its second matra उम्

**5.4** However some men wish for bigger roles than that.

By sincerely practicing and meditating on
- the first matra अम् with attention on the Manipura Chakra at the Navel, and also
- the second matra उम् with attention on the Anahata Chakra at the Heart

the cosmic laws get revealed as described in the Yajurveda. The practical mind becomes sharp. Physics and Chemistry become well understood.

Thereby a person's talents and yearnings propel him to achieve success in the entire solar system planetary domain. He is hailed by diverse denizens and life forms while maintaining his home and connections on planet Earth.

यः पुनरेतं त्रिमात्रेणोमित्येतेनैवाक्षरेण परं पुरुषमभिध्यायीत स तेजसि सूर्ये सम्पन्नः । यथा पादोदरस्त्वचा विनिर्भुच्यत एवं ह वै स पाप्मना विनिर्भुक्तः स सामभिरुन्नीयते ब्रह्मलोकं स एतस्माज्जीवघनात्परात्परं पुरिशयं पुरुषमीक्षते तदेतौ श्लोकौ भवतः ॥ ५.५

yaḥ punaretaṃ trimātreṇomityetenaivākṣareṇa paraṃ puruṣamabhidhyāyīta sa tejasi sūrye sampannaḥ |

yathā pādodarastvacā vinirbhucyata evaṃ ha vai sa pāpmanā vinirbhuktaḥ sa sāmabhirunnīyate brahmalokaṃ sa etasmājjīvaghanātparātparaṃ puriśayaṃ puruṣamīkṣate tadetau ślokau bhavataḥ ‖  5.5

पुनः Moreover, यः एतं त्रिमात्रेण अभिध्यायीत ॐ, इति, the one who would likewise practice meditation on this first, second, and third matra of OM, एतेन अक्षरेण परं पुरुषम् by this imperishable, the transcendental Being, सः he तेजसि in the effulgent सूर्ये milky way of the sun सम्पन्नः becomes provided for.

यथा पादोदरः त्वचा विनिर्मुच्यते Just as a serpent sheds its skin in its process of growth – sloughing –, एवं ह वै सः पाप्मना विनिर्मुक्तः । Likewise verily he drops his mind's baggage of grief, turmoil, conflict and hatred.

सामभिः By the hymns of the Samaveda सः his spirit ब्रह्मलोकम् to the galactic domain उन्नीयते expands till.

एतस्मात् Hence सः जीवघनात् ईक्षते he becomes wise to the collective spirit. He now recognizes fully परं the transcendental पुरुषम् godly Being पुरिशयम् deep in the recesses of the heart in his own sprawling body-City.

## OM - its third matra मम्

$5.5$ Rarely enough, do men seek far bigger workplaces.

By sincerely practicing and meditating in sequence on
- the first matra अम् with attention on the Manipura Chakra at the Navel,
- the second matra उम् with attention on the Anahata Chakra at the Heart,
- the third matra मम् with attention on the Ajna Chakra between the Eyebrows

the quantum cosmic laws get revealed as described in the Samaveda. The spirit gets supremely elevated. The farthest regions of creation open up to welcome. Space, Light, Sound, Gravity, Time; are all mastered.

Thereby a person's talents and yearnings propel him to achieve success in the entire solar system planetary domain. He is hailed by diverse denizens and life forms while maintaining his home and connections on planet Earth.

---

तत् एतौ श्लोकौ भवतः ॥ that is the essence of this verse which is also elucidated in the next two verses.

तिस्रो मात्रा मृत्युमत्यः प्रयुक्ता अन्योन्यसक्ता अनविप्रयुक्ताः ।
क्रियासु बाह्यान्तरमध्यमासु सम्यक्प्रयुक्तासु न कम्पते ज्ञः ॥ ५.६

tisro mātrā mṛtyumatyaḥ prayuktā anyonyasaktā
anaviprayuktāḥ | kriyāsu bāhyāntaramadhyamāsu
samyakprayuktāsu na kampate jñaḥ ॥  5.6

तिस्रः मात्राः मृत्युमत्यः प्रयुक्ताः अन्योन्यसक्ताः अनविप्रयुक्ताः ।
क्रियासु बाह्यान्तरमध्यमासु सम्यक् प्रयुक्तासु न कम्पते ज्ञः ॥ ५.६

तिस्रः the three मात्राः matras एकैकशः one at a time
प्रयुक्ताः practiced and used चेत् मृत्युमत्यः give benefits
that are relative and approximate in the SPACE-TIME
domain.

अन्योन्यसक्ताः When done methodically in sequence
अनविप्रयुक्ताः as learnt properly from a Master
बाह्य-आभ्यन्तर–मध्यमासु with the body-mind-breath
क्रियासु in tandem and well-aligned,
सम्यक् प्रयुक्तासु in harmony and with pure intent,

Then ज्ञः the one having knowledge and skill
न कम्पते does not waver from his status, is never
tempted to go for distracting pleasures, does not fall
from grace.

# OM - its connecting ardha matra

**5.6** The proper chanting of OM and by deeply meditating on the sacred sound establishes the ardha matra, or its divinity, that underlies and connects.

It is what shapes our notions and makes the intellect mature. It is which keeps us away from harm.

Saints have taught that ॐ consists of A, U, M matras, and the <u>invisible unheard ardha matra</u>, permeating all.

ऋग्भिरेतं यजुर्भिरन्तरिक्षं सामभिर्यत्तत्कवयो वेदयन्ते ।

तमोङ्कारेणैवायतनेनान्वेति विद्वान् यत्तच्छान्तमजरममृतमभयं परं चेति

॥ ५.७

ṛgbhiretaṃ yajurbhirantarikṣaṃ sāmabhiryattatkavayo vedayante | tamoṅkāreṇaivāyatanenānveti vidvān yattacchāntamajaramamṛtamabhayaṃ paraṃ ceti ॥ 5.7

ऋग्भिः एतं यजुर्भिः अन्तरिक्षं सामभिः यत् तत् कवयः वेदयन्ते । तम् ॐकारेण एव आयतनेन अन्वेति विद्वान् यत् तत् शान्तम् अजरम् अमृतम् अभयं परं च इति ॥

5.7 ऋग्भिः एतं By the mastery of Rigveda - this humility of Earth is achieved,
यजुर्भिः अन्तरिक्षं by mastery of Yajurveda – the trust of the Solar System is got,
यत् कवयः वेदयन्ते as known by the learned wise men
सामभिः तत् ब्रह्मलोकम् आप्नोति by mastery of Samaveda – the freedom to function and travel in the entire Galaxy is gained.

It is Guru Grace that keeps the mind innocent and free of bias - that is the underlying achievement of it all – that is what is really worthy of attainment.

यत् Since that grace bestows:
शान्तम् अजरम् peaceful acceptance and fortitude in old age,
अमृतम् अभयं परं a cheerful fearlessness at all times in all situations.

तं The विद्वान् wise person ॐ–कारेण by the sacred syllable OM आयतनेन by the practice of its techniques and deep meditations,

एव अन्वेति definitely achieves union with the Divine.

च इति ॥ and full stop. And End of class. The teaching is till here.

# 6<sup>th</sup> Question by Sukeśā

## Who is the Being with 16 attributes?
Ofcourse Oneself.

## Sixteen Attributes of Being

The fully blossomed human being with the 5 elements in harmony, the 5 vayus functioning smoothly, the 5 senses turned inward, and the mind merged in the Divine.


अथ हैनं सुकेशा भारद्वाजः पप्रच्छ । भगवन् हिरण्यनाभः कौसल्यो राजपुत्रो मामुपेत्यैतं प्रश्नमपृच्छत । षोडशकलं भारद्वाज पुरुषं वेत्थ तमहं कुमारमब्रुवं नाहमिमं वेद यद्यहमिममवेदिषं कथं ते नावक्ष्यमिति समूलो वा एष परिशुष्यति योऽनृतमभिवदति तस्मान्नार्हाम्यनृतं वक्तुं स तूष्णीं रथमारुह्य प्रवव्राज । तं त्वा पृच्छामि क्वासौ पुरुष इति ॥ ६.१

atha hainaṃ sukeśā bhāradvājaḥ papraccha | bhagavan hiraṇyanābhaḥ kausalyo rājaputro māmupetyaitaṃ praśnamaprcchata | ṣoḍaśakalam bhāradvāja puruṣaṃ vettha tamahaṃ kumāramabruvaṃ nāhamimaṃ veda yadyahamimamavediṣam kathaṃ te nāvakṣyamiti samūlo vā eṣa pariśuṣyati yo'nṛtamabhivadati tasmānnārhāmyanṛtaṃ vaktuṃ sa tūṣṇīṃ rathamāruhya pravavrāja | taṃ tvā prcchāmi kvāsau puruṣa iti || 6.1

अथ ह भारद्वाजः सुकेशा एनं पप्रच्छ भगवन् कौसल्यः हिरण्यनाभः राजपुत्रः माम् उपेत्य एतं प्रश्नं पप्रच्छ भारद्वाज षोडशकलं पुरुषं वेत्थ अहं तं कुमारम् अब्रुवम् अहम् इमं न वेद । अहं यदि इमम् अवेदिषं तर्हि ते कथम् न अवक्ष्यम् इति । यः अनृतं वदति एषः वै समूलः परिशुष्यति तस्मात् अनृतं वक्तुं न अर्हामि । सः तूष्णीम् रथम् आरुह्य प्रववाज त्वा तं पृच्छामि असौ पुरुषः क्व इति ॥

**6.1** Finally love has smitten. A prince is asking;
the prince who is hoping to fall in love.

Clothing his quest in the number sixteen. Sweet
sixteen, an attraction, the pull of love is hidden in
this quest.

Initially we might fall in love with something pretty,
something small, just a toy or a toffee.

Later when the intellect expands and the heart
ripens, one only seeks love within!
*(though one may wish for an external confirmation)*

- Pain of truth leads to liberation.
- Lack is shockingly painful.
- Not denying the lack sparks the journey for
  fulfillment.

## 5 Elements+5 Prana Vayu+5 Senses+Mind

What has been studied earlier has been summarized
here in the last question. We have seen in detail the
- five Elements – space, air, light, water, earth
- five Vayus – prana, apana, vyana, samana, udana
- five Senses – sound, touch, sight, taste, smell
- one Mind – that rules all and is ruled by all

तस्मै स होवाच । इहैवान्तःशरीरे सोम्य स पुरुषो यस्मिन्नेताः षोडश कलाः प्रभवन्तीति ॥ ६.२

tasmai sa hovāca | ihaivāntaḥśarīre somya sa puruṣo yasminnetāḥ ṣoḍaśa kalāḥ prabhavantīti || 6.2

तस्मै to them सः he ह उवाच I spoke. इह here एव only अन्तःशरीरे in the entire body सोम्य O Child! सः he पुरुषः the Supreme (dwells), यस्मिन् in whom एताः these षोडश sixteen कलाः attributes प्रभवन्ति appear and be इति ॥

स ईक्षांचक्रे । कस्मिन्नहमुत्क्रान्त उत्क्रान्तो भविष्यामि कस्मिन् वा प्रतिष्ठिते प्रतिष्ठास्यामीति ॥ ६.३

sa īkṣāṃcakre | kasminnahamutkrānta utkrānto bhaviṣyāmi kasmin vā pratiṣṭhite pratiṣṭhāsyāmīti || 6.3

सः The ईक्षांचक्रे I supreme contemplated –
कस्मिन् how may अहम् । उत्क्रान्ते expanding उत्क्रान्तः expansive भविष्यामि become,
कस्मिन् वा likewise how प्रतिष्ठिते stilling and silently प्रतिष्ठास्यामि stillness – a point be, इति ॥ thus.

**6.2** That Being you are seeking, resides within this same body, whether yours or mine.

**6.3** The Being intelligently devised a formula whereby it could stay in peace, and depart at will.

स प्राणमसृजत प्राणाच्छ्रद्धां खं वायुज्र्योतिरापः पृथिवीन्द्रियं मनः ।
अन्नमन्नाद् वीर्यं तपो मन्त्राः कर्मलोका लोकेषु च नाम च ॥ ६.४
sa prāṇamasṛjata prāṇacchraddhāṃ khaṃ vāyurjyotirāpaḥ
pṛthivīndriyaṃ manaḥ | annamannād vīryaṃ tapo
mantrāḥ karmalokā lokeṣu ca nāma ca || 6.4

सः he प्राणम् the vital life force असृजत created, प्राणात् from the breath श्रद्धां intense trust खं space वायुः air ज्योतिः light आपः water पृथिवी earth इन्द्रियं senses मनः mind अन्नम् । food.

अन्नात् from nourishment वीर्यं strength and stamina तपः hard work and discipline मन्त्राः tools and methods and techniques कर्म work, act, endeavor, aim लोकाः । universes, galaxies, planes with diverse laws and beings.

लोकेषु च नाम च ॥ in the universes, names, identities, feeling of mineness and distinction.

**6.4** The formula structure:

Life force to begin with, that gives life
- to emotions e.g. Faith and Trust
- to the elements space, air, light, water, earth
- to the senses
- to the mind and its components
- to the food chain

The food chain helps sustain
- strength and vitality
- routine and discipline
- reading, learning, and media
- works, activity, and engagements
- diverse cultures, races, lands and aliens

The diverse cultures having distinct names, independent personalities, aims and ideals.

स यथेमा नद्यः स्यन्दमानाः समुद्रायणाः समुद्रं प्राप्यास्तं गच्छन्ति
भिद्येते तासां नामरूपे समुद्र इत्येवं प्रोच्यते । एवमेवास्य परिद्रष्टुरिमाः
षोडश कलाः पुरुषायणाः पुरुषं प्राप्यास्तं गच्छन्ति भिद्येते चाऽऽसां
नामरूपे पुरुष इत्येवं प्रोच्यते स एषोऽकलोऽमृतो भवति तदेष श्लोकः
॥ ६.५

sa yathemā nadyaḥ syandamānāḥ samudrāyaṇāḥ
samudraṃ prāpyāstam gacchanti bhidyete tāsāṃ
nāmarūpe samudra ityevaṃ procyate | evamevāsya
paridraṣṭurimāḥ ṣoḍaśa kalāḥ puruṣāyaṇāḥ puruṣam
prāpyāstam gacchanti bhidyete cā''sāṃ nāmarūpe
puruṣa ityevaṃ procyate sa eṣo'kalo'mṛto bhavati
tadeṣa ślokaḥ || 6.5


यथा just as इमाः all these नद्यः streams स्यन्दमानाः  flowing
समुद्रायणाः towards the ocean, प्राप्य having अस्तं merged
समुद्रं with the ocean गच्छन्ति disappear, भिद्येते obliterate तासां
their नामरूपे individual name and form identities,
सः समुद्रः The ocean इति thus एवं only प्रोच्यते । it is then
called.
एवम् एव likewise अस्य of this परिद्रष्टुः visionary इमाः these
षोडश sixteen कलाः attributes पुरुषायणाः dissolving in the
Supreme Consciousness पुरुषं प्राप्य अस्तं गच्छन्ति disappear
having merged with the Brahman भिद्येते च आसां नामरूपे and
erased their identities,
पुरुषः Brahman इति thus एवं alone प्रोच्यते it is called,
सः he एषः this अकलः attributeless अमृतः imperishable भवति
। becomes. तत् एषः श्लोकः further explained in next verse ॥

## 6.5 How the formula works perfectly – an analogy:

Just as many streams, rivers, rivulets, water buckets, raindrops, and drains too, all flow down to the ocean; and once there they all lose themselves. Their independent identity no longer persists. It is all simply Ocean.

Likewise, the senses, elements, pancha prana vayu, bodies, minds, and the rest, whether cosmic dust or living beings, or anything else, when these merge in Brahman the infinite, there is naught else, simply the Infinite Brahman.

अरा इव रथनाभौ कला यस्मिन् प्रतिष्ठिताः ।
तं वेद्यं पुरुषं वेद यथा मा वो मृत्युः परिव्यथा इति ॥ ६.६

arā iva rathanābhau kalā yasmin pratiṣṭhitāḥ | taṃ vedyaṃ puruṣaṃ veda yathā mā vo mṛtyuḥ parivyathā iti ॥ 6.6

इव Just as अराः spokes रथनाभौ in the chariot wheel (are well fitted, similarly) कलाः all divine virtues यस्मिन् in which प्रतिष्ठिताः । are well ingrained.

तं that वेद्यं worth aiming, studying, and attaining पुरुषं Supreme Consciousness वेद you must endeavor for,

यथा if मृत्युः frustration, emptiness, desolateness मा may not वः your परिव्यथाः life lay waste. इति ॥

## 6.6 Another analogy to drive the point home.

In a fast moving chariot, the spokes of the wheel are all a blur, the fan blades become transparent, matter dissolves in thin air.

Likewise when the movie stops, only the pure white screen remains.

When one realizes the Truth, all dissimilarities, polarities, and grievances fade, death becomes a passing fad.

No longer doth worry haunt, nor fear remain.

Hence make It your foremost priority to delve into the illuminating scriptures at the feet of the Master, so that your life may blossom and you may enjoy great peace and happiness.

तान् होवाचैतावदेवाहमेतत्परं ब्रह्म वेद । नातः परमस्तीति ॥ ६.७

tān hovācaitāvadevāhametatparaṃ brahma veda | nātaḥ paramastīti ॥ 6.7

तान् To them ह (*with love in his voice*)उवाच he concluded -

एतावत् this is all एव completely what अहम् । एतत् regarding THE परं transcendental ब्रह्म Brahman वेद । know.

न Nothing अतः surpassing परम् beyond अस्ति it is.

इति ॥ I conclude here finally.

---

ते तमर्चयन्तस्त्वं हि नः पिता योऽस्माकमविद्यायाः परं पारं तारयसीति । नमः परमऋषिभ्यो नमः परमऋषिभ्यः ॥ ६.८

te tamarcayantastvaṃ hi naḥ pitā yo'smākamavidyāyāḥ paraṃ pāraṃ tārayasīti | namaḥ paramarṣibhyo namaḥ paramarṣibhyaḥ ॥ 6.8

ते They the six seekers तम् to him the Master अर्चयन्तः devotedly bowed saying - त्वं Thou art हि (*quivering with emotion, tears running down their cheeks*)नः our पिता most respected guardian. यः Thou who hath अस्माकम् of ours अविद्यायाः the shroud of dense notions, fears, misunderstood concepts and narrow vision तारयसि completely shred and cleared, and परं पारं इति । established us in the transcendental loving joyful divinity. नमः परमऋषिभ्यः नमः परमऋषिभ्यः ॥ Heartfelt Gratefulness.

## 6.7 The Master sums up:

Long and True has been our Satsang, our association
has surely elucidated and revealed the Divine.

Purer than Divinity naught any,
Higher than its attainment no aim.


## 6.8 The satiated disciples exult gratefully:

O Super Soul! Thee art surely our beloved parent.
Thee hath cast us beyond all dangers-clutches.
Thee have taken us safely home.

Loving prostrations! Wholehearted obeisance.


Aren't we all seeking Love?
Prashna ends on this poignant note.

# Etymology of Upanishad

व्युत्पत्ति
Consider Adi Shankaracharya's derivation of the
word 'Upanishad' as given in his bhashyam on the
Katha Upanishad.

उप + नि + षद् + क्विप् –> उपनिषद्

The Sanskrit root from Dhatupatha 1c - 854, 6c - 1427
षद्ॢ विशरण–गति–अवसादनेषु has the three meanings,
namely विशरण= wither, गति= attain, अवसादनं = sit.

In the context of wisdom, we can say
* wither away one's stupidity
* attain liberation
* sit with a conviction

The upasarga उप stands for nearness, closeness.
The upasarga नि stands for delving into, intense
The pratyaya क्विप् makes a noun, and while joining,
it vanishes entirely.

Thus the word 'Upanishad' is formed, and it has the
meaning of destroying one's ignorance and gaining
freedom, when we sit devotedly at the feet of the
Master.

# Latin Transliteration Chart

International Alphabet of Sanskrit Transliteration (I.A.S.T.)

| a | ā | i | ī | u | ū | ṛ | ṝ | ḷ | | |
|---|---|---|---|---|---|---|---|---|---|---|
| अ | आ | इ | ई | उ | ऊ | ऋ | ॠ | ऌ | | |
| | | | | | | ◌ृ | ◌ॄ | ◌ॢ | | |
| e | ai | o | au | ṃ | m̐ | ḥ | Ardha Visarga | oṃ | | |
| ए | ऐ | ओ | औ | ◌ं | ◌ँ | ◌: | □ | ॐ | | |

Consonants are shown with vowel 'a= अ' for uttering

| ka | क | ca | च | ṭa | ट | ta | त | | pa | प |
|----|---|----|---|----|---|----|---|---|----|---|
| kha | ख | cha | छ | ṭha | ठ | tha | थ | | pha | फ |
| ga | ग | ja | ज | ḍa | ड | da | द | | ba | ब |
| gha | घ | jha | झ | ḍha | ढ | dha | ध | | bha | भ |
| ṅa | ङ | ña | ञ | ṇa | ण | na | न | | ma | म |
| | | | | | | | | | | |
| ya | ra | la | va | | ḷa | ' | | | | |
| य | र | ल | व | | ळ | S | | | | |
| | | | | Consonant only | | | | | | |
| śa | ṣa | sa | ha | | ka | क्अ = क | | | | |
| श | ष | स | ह | | k | क् | | | | |

The symbol ꣳ is pronounced as गुं guṃ. It is an ayogavaha अयोगवाह sound seen in Vedic literature due to Sandhi.

# Verses for Chanting

Accents used in Sanskrit verses increase the power and flow of the mantras during chanting.

Anudatta ○̣= अनुदात्तः = signifies base pitch.

Udatta = उदात्तः = unmarked, standard pitch.

Svarita´ = स्वरितः = high pitch.

Dirgha Svarita˝ =दीर्घः  स्वरितः=high to low to normal pitch

॥ अथ अथर्ववेदीय प्रश्नोपनिषद् ॥

शान्तिपाठः


ॐ भद्रं कर्णेभिः श्रृणुयाम देवाः । भद्रं पश्ये माक्षभिरु यजत्राः ।
स्थिरैरङ्गैस् तुष्टुवाꣳ सस्तनूभिः । व्यशेम देवहितं यदायुः । स्वस्ति न
इन्द्रो वृद्धश्रवाः । स्वस्ति नः पूषा विश्ववेदाः । स्वस्ति नस्ताक्ष्यों
अरिष्टनेमिः । स्वस्ति नो बृहस्पतिर्दधातु ॥ ॐ शान्तिः  शान्तिः
शान्तिः ॥


प्रथमः प्रश्नः ॐ

सुकेशा च भारद्वाजः शैब्यश्च सत्यकामः सौर्यायणी च गार्ग्यः
कौसल्यश्चाश्वलायनो भार्गवो वैदर्भिः कबन्धी कात्यायनस्ते हैते ब्रह्मपरा
ब्रह्मनिष्ठाः परं ब्रह्मान्वेषमाणा एष ह वै तत्सर्वं वक्ष्यतीति ते ह समित्पाणयो
भगवन्तं पिप्पलादमुपसन्नाः ॥ १.१

तान् ह स ऋषिरुवाच भूय एव तपसा ब्रह्मचर्येण श्रद्धया संवत्सरं संवत्स्यथ
यथाकामं प्रश्नान् पृच्छत यदि विज्ञास्यामः सर्वं ह वो वक्ष्याम इति ॥ १.२

अथ कबन्धी कात्यायन उपेत्य पप्रच्छ ।

भगवन् कुतो ह वा इमाः प्रजाः प्रजायन्त इति ॥ १.३

तस्मै स होवाच प्रजाकामो वै प्रजापतिः स तपोऽतप्यत स तपस् तप्त्वा स
मिथुनमुत्पादयते । रयिं च प्राणं चेत्येतौ मे बहुधा प्रजाः करिष्यत इति ॥ १.४

आदित्यो ह वै प्राणो रयिरेव चन्द्रमा रयिर्वा एतत् सर्वं यन्मूर्तं चामूर्तं च तस्मान्मूर्तिरेव रयिः ॥ १.५

अथादित्य उदयन् यत् प्राचीं दिशं प्रविशति तेन प्राच्यान् प्राणान् रश्मिषु सन्निधत्ते । यद् दक्षिणां यत् प्रतीचीं यदुदीचीं यदधो यदूर्ध्वं यदन्तरा दिशो यत्सर्वं प्रकाशयति तेन सर्वान् प्राणान् रश्मिषु सन्निधत्ते ॥ १.६

स एष वैश्वानरो विश्वरूपः प्राणोऽग्निरुदयते ।

तदेतदु ऋचाऽभ्युक्तम् ॥ १.७

विश्वरूपं हरिणं जातवेदसं परायणं ज्योतिरेकं तपन्तम् ।

सहस्ररश्मिः शतधा वर्तमानः प्राणः प्रजानामुदयत्येष सूर्यः ॥ १.८

संवत्सरो वै प्रजापतिस्तस्यायने दक्षिणं चोत्तरं च । तद्ये ह वै तदिष्टापूर्ते कृतमित्युपासते । ते चान्द्रमसमेव लोकमभिजयन्ते । त एव पुनरावर्तन्ते तस्मादेते ऋषयः प्रजाकामा दक्षिणं प्रतिपद्यन्ते । एष ह वै रयिर्यः पितृयाणः ॥ १.९

अथोत्तरेण तपसा ब्रह्मचर्येण श्रद्धया विद्ययात्मानमन्विष्यादित्यमभिजयन्ते ।

एतद्वै प्राणानामायतनमेतदमृतमभयमेतत् परायणमेतस्मान्न पुनरावर्तन्त इत्येष निरोधः । तदेष श्लोकः ॥ १.१०

पञ्चपादं पितरं द्वादशाकृतिं दिव आहुः परे अर्धे पुरीषिणम् ।

अथेमे अन्य उ परे विचक्षणं सप्तचक्रे षडर आहुरर्पितमिति ॥ १.११

मासो वै प्रजापतिस्तस्य कृष्णपक्ष एव रयिः शुक्लः प्राणस्तस्मादेते ऋषयः शुक्ल इष्टं कुर्वन्तीतर इतरस्मिन् ॥ १.१२

अहोरात्रो वै प्रजापतिस्तस्याहरेव प्राणो रात्रिरेव रयिः । प्राणं वा एते प्रस्कन्दन्ति ये दिवा रत्या संयुज्यन्ते ब्रह्मचर्यमेव तद्यद्रात्रौ रत्या संयुज्यन्ते ॥ १.१३

अन्नं वै प्रजापतिस्ततो ह वै तद्रेतस्तस्मादिमाः प्रजाः प्रजायन्त इति ॥ १.१४

तद्ये ह वै तत्प्रजापतिव्रतं चरन्ति ते मिथुनमुत्पादयन्ते ।

तेषामेवैष ब्रह्मलोको येषां तपो ब्रह्मचर्यं येषु सत्यं प्रतिष्ठितम् ॥ १.१५

तेषामसौ विरजो ब्रह्मलोको न येषु जिह्ममनृतं न माया चेति ॥ १.१६

अथ हैनं भार्गवो वैदर्भिः पप्रच्छ । भगवन् कत्येव देवाः प्रजां विधारयन्ते
कतर एतत्प्रकाशयन्ते कः पुनरेषां वरिष्ठ इति ॥ २.१

तस्मै स होवाचाकाशो ह वा एष देवो वायुरग्निरापः पृथिवी वाङ्मनश्चक्षुः
श्रोत्रं च । ते प्रकाश्याभिवदन्ति वयमेतद्बाणमवष्टभ्य विधारयामः ॥ २.२

तान् वरिष्ठः प्राण उवाच । मा मोहमापद्यथ अहमेवैतत्पञ्चधात्मानं
प्रविभज्यैतद्बाणमवष्टभ्य विधारयामीति तेऽश्रद्धाना बभूवुः ॥ २.३

सोऽभिमानादूर्ध्वमुत्क्रमत इव तस्मिन्नुत्क्रामत्यथेतरे सर्व एवोत्क्रामन्ते
तस्मिंश्च प्रतिष्ठमाने सर्व एव प्रतिष्ठन्ते । तद्यथा मक्षिका
मधुकरराजानमुत्क्रामन्तं सर्व एवोत्क्रामन्ते तस्मिंश्च प्रतिष्ठमाने सर्वा एव
प्रतिष्ठन्त एवं वाङ्मनश्चक्षुः श्रोत्रं च ते प्रीताः प्राणं स्तुन्वन्ति ॥ २.४

एषोऽग्निस्तपत्येष सूर्य एष पर्जन्यो मघवानेष वायुः ।
एष पृथिवी रयिर्देवः सदसच्चामृतं च यत् ॥ २.५

अरा इव रथनाभौ प्राणे सर्वं प्रतिष्ठितम् ।
ऋचो यजूंषि सामानि यज्ञः क्षत्रं ब्रह्म च ॥ २.६

प्रजापतिश्चरसि गर्भे त्वमेव प्रतिजायसे ।
तुभ्यं प्राण प्रजास्त्विमा बलिं हरन्ति यः प्राणैः प्रतितिष्ठसि ॥ २.७

देवानामसि वह्नितमः पितृणां प्रथमा स्वधा ।
ऋषीणां चरितं सत्यमथर्वाङ्गिरसामसि ॥ २.८

इन्द्रस्त्वं प्राण तेजसा रुद्रोऽसि परिरक्षिता ।
त्वमन्तरिक्षे चरसि सूर्यस्त्वं ज्योतिषां पतिः ॥ २.९

यदा त्वमभिवर्षस्यथेमाः प्राण ते प्रजाः ।
आनन्दरूपास्तिष्ठन्ति कामायान्नं भविष्यतीति ॥ २.१०

व्रात्यस्त्वं प्राणैकर्षिरत्ता विश्वस्य सत्पतिः ।
वयमाद्यस्य दातारः पिता त्वं मातरिश्व नः ॥ २.११

या ते तनूर्वाचि प्रतिष्ठिता या श्रोत्रे या च चक्षुषि ।
या च मनसि सन्तता शिवां तां कुरु मोत्क्रमीः ॥ २.१२

प्राणस्येदं वशे सर्वं त्रिदिवे यत् प्रतिष्ठितम् ।

मातेव पुत्रान् रक्षस्व श्रीश्च प्रज्ञां च विधेहि न इति ॥ २.१३

तृतीयः प्रश्नः

अथ हैनं कौसल्यश्चाऽऽश्वलायनः पप्रच्छ ।

भगवन् कुत एष प्राणो जायते कथमायात्यस्मिञ्छरीर आत्मानं वा प्रविभज्य

कथं प्रतिष्ठते केनोत्क्रमते कथं बाह्यमभिधत्ते कथमध्यात्ममिति ॥ ३.१

तस्मै स होवाचातिप्रश्नान् पृच्छसि ब्रह्मिष्ठोऽसीति तस्मात्तेऽहं ब्रवीमि ॥ ३.२

आत्मन एष प्राणो जायते । यथैषा पुरुषे छायैतस्मिन्नेतदाततं

मनोकृतेनायात्यस्मिञ्छरीरे ॥ ३.३

यथा सम्राडेवाधिकृतान् विनियुङ्क्ते । एतान् ग्रामानेतान्

ग्रामानधितिष्ठस्वेत्येवमेवैष प्राण इतरान् प्राणान् पृथक्पृथगेव सन्निधत्ते ॥ ३.४

पायूपस्थेऽपानं चक्षुःश्रोत्रे मुखनासिकाभ्यां प्राणः स्वयं प्रातिष्ठते मध्ये तु

समानः । एष ह्येतद्धुतमन्नं समं नयति तस्मादेताः सप्तार्चिषो भवन्ति ॥ ३.५

हृदि ह्येष आत्मा । अत्रैतदेकशतं नाडीनां तासां शतं शतमेकैकस्यां

द्वासप्ततिर्द्वासप्ततिः प्रतिशाखानाडीसहस्राणि भवन्त्यासु व्यानश्चरति ॥ ३.६

अथैकयोर्ध्व उदानः पुण्येन पुण्यं लोकं नयति

पापेन पापमुभाभ्यामेव मनुष्यलोकम् ॥ ३.७

आदित्यो ह वै बाह्यः प्राण उदयत्येष ह्येनं चाक्षुषं प्राणमनुगृह्णानः ।

पृथिव्यां या देवता सैषा पुरुषस्यापानमवष्टभ्यान्तरा यदाकाशः स समानो

वायुर्व्यानः ॥ ३.८

तेजो ह वा उदानस्तस्मादुपशान्ततेजाः ।

पुनर्भवमिन्द्रियैर्मनसि सम्पद्यमानैः ॥ ३.९

यच्चित्तस्तेनैष प्राणमायाति प्राणस्तेजसा युक्तः ।

सहात्मना यथासङ्कल्पितं लोकं नयति ॥ ३.१०

य एवं विद्वान् प्राणं वेद ।

न हास्य प्रजा हीयतेऽमृतो भवति तदेषः श्लोकः ॥ ३.११

उत्पत्तिमायति स्थानं विभुत्वं चैव पञ्चधा । अध्यात्मं चैव प्राणस्य
विज्ञायामृतमश्नुते विज्ञायामृतमश्नुत इति ॥ ३.१२

<u>चतुर्थः प्रश्नः</u>

अथ हैनं सौर्यायणी गार्ग्यः पप्रच्छ । भगवन्नेतस्मिन् पुरुषे कानि स्वपन्ति
कान्यस्मिञ्जाग्रति कतर एष देवः स्वप्नान् पश्यति कस्यैतत्सुखं भवति कस्मिन्नु
सर्वे सम्प्रतिष्ठिता भवन्तीति ॥ ४.१

तस्मै स होवाच । यथा गार्ग्य मरीचयोऽर्कस्यास्तं गच्छतः सर्वा
एतस्मिंस्तेजोमण्डल एकीभवन्ति । ताः पुनः पुनरुदयतः प्रचरन्त्येवं ह वै
तत्सर्वं परे देवे मनस्येकीभवति । तेन तर्ह्येष पुरुषो न शृणोति न पश्यति न
जिघ्रति न रसयते न स्पृशते नाभिवदते नादत्ते नानन्दयते न विसृजते नेयायते
स्वपितीत्याचक्षते ॥ ४.२

प्राणाग्नय एवैतस्मिन् पुरे जाग्रति । गार्हपत्यो ह वा एषोऽपानो
व्यानोऽन्वाहार्यपचनो यद् गार्हपत्यात् प्रणीयते प्रणयनादाहवनीयः प्राणः ॥
४.३

यदुच्छ्वासनिःश्वासावेतावाहुती समं नयतीति स समानः । मनो ह वाव
यजमानः । इष्टफलमेवोदानः । स एनं यजमानमहरहर्ब्रह्म गमयति ॥ ४.४

अत्रैष देवः स्वप्ने महिमानमनुभवति । यद् दृष्टं दृष्टमनुपश्यति श्रुतं
श्रुतमेवार्थमनुशृणोति देशदिगन्तरैश्च प्रत्यनुभूतं पुनः पुनः प्रत्यनुभवति दृष्टं
चादृष्टं च श्रुतं चाश्रुतं चानुभूतं चाननुभूतं च सच्चासच्च सर्वं पश्यति सर्वः
पश्यति ॥ ४.५

स यदा तेजसाऽभिभूतो भवति । अत्रैष देवः स्वप्नान् न पश्यत्यथ
यदैतस्मिञ्छरीरे एतत्सुखं भवति ॥ ४.६

स यथा सोम्य वयांसि वसोवृक्षं सम्प्रतिष्ठन्ते एवं ह वै तत्सर्वं पर आत्मनि
सम्प्रतिष्ठते ॥ ४.७

पृथिवी च पृथिवीमात्रा चापश्चापोमात्रा च तेजश्च तेजोमात्रा च वायुश्च
वायुमात्रा चाकाशश्चाकाशमात्रा च चक्षुश्च द्रष्टव्यं च श्रोत्रं च श्रोतव्यं च घ्राणं

च घ्रातव्यं च रसश्च रसयितव्यं च त्वक्च स्पर्शयितव्यं च वाक्च वक्तव्यं च
हस्तौ चादातव्यं चोपस्थश्चानन्दयितव्यं च पायुश्च विसर्जयितव्यं च पादौ च
गन्तव्यं च मनश्च मन्तव्यं च बुद्धिश्च बोद्धव्यं चाहङ्कारश्चाहङ्कर्तव्यं च चित्तं च
चेतयितव्यं च तेजश्च विद्योतयितव्यं च प्राणश्च विद्यारयितव्यं च ॥ ४.८

एष हि द्रष्टा स्प्रष्टा श्रोता घ्राता रसयिता मन्ता बोद्धा कर्ता विज्ञानात्मा पुरुषः ।
स परेऽक्षर आत्मनि सम्प्रतिष्ठते ॥ ४.९

परमेवाक्षरं प्रतिपद्यते स यो ह वै तदच्छायमशरीरमलोहितं शुभ्रमक्षरं वेदयते
यस्तु सोम्य । स सर्वज्ञः सर्वो भवति । तदेष श्लोकः ॥ ४.१०

विज्ञानात्मा सह देवैश्च सर्वैः प्राणा भूतानि सम्प्रतिष्ठन्ति यत्र ।
तदक्षरं वेदयते यस्तु सोम्य स सर्वज्ञः सर्वमेवाविवेशेति ॥ ४.११


<u>पञ्चमः प्रश्नः</u>

अथ हैनं शैब्यः सत्यकामः पप्रच्छ । स यो ह वै तद् भगवन् मनुष्येषु
प्रायणान्तमोङ्कारमभिध्यायीत । कतमं वाव स तेन लोकं जयतीति तस्मै स
होवाच ॥ ५.१

एतद् वै सत्यकाम परं चापरं च ब्रह्म यदोङ्कारः । तस्माद् विद्वान्
एतेनैवाऽऽयतनेनैकतरमन्वेति ॥ ५.२

स यद्येकमात्रमभिध्यायीत स तेनैव संवेदितस्तूर्णमेव जगत्यामभिसम्पद्यते ।
तमृचो मनुष्यलोकमुपनयन्ते स तत्र तपसा ब्रह्मचर्येण श्रद्धया सम्पन्नो
महिमानमनुभवति ॥ ५.३

अथ यदि द्विमात्रेण मनसि सम्पद्यते सोऽन्तरिक्षं यजुर्भिरुन्नीयते सोमलोकम् ।
स सोमलोके विभूतिमनुभूय पुनरावर्तते ॥ ५.४

यः पुनरेतं त्रिमात्रेणोमित्येतेनैवाक्षरेण परं पुरुषमभिध्यायीत स तेजसि सूर्ये
सम्पन्नः । यथा पादोदरस्त्वचा विनिर्भुच्यत एवं ह वै स पाप्मना विनिर्भुक्तः स
सामभिरुन्नीयते ब्रह्मलोकं स एतस्माज्जीवघनात्परात्परं पुरिशयं पुरुषमीक्षते
तदेतौ श्लोकौ भवतः ॥ ५.५

तिस्रो मात्रा मृत्युमत्यः प्रयुक्ता अन्योन्यसक्ता अनविप्रयुक्ताः ।

क्रियासु बाह्यान्तरमध्यमासु सम्यक्प्रयुक्तासु न कम्पते ज्ञः ॥ ५.६

ऋग्भिरेतं यजुर्भिरन्तरिक्षं सामभिर्यत्तत्कवयो वेदयन्ते ।

तमोङ्कारेणैवायतनेनान्वेति विद्वान् यत्तच्छान्तमजरममृतमभयं परं चेति ॥

५.७

<u>षष्ठः प्रश्नः</u>

अथ हैनं सुकेशा भारद्वाजः पप्रच्छ । भगवन् हिरण्यनाभः कौसल्यो राजपुत्रो

मामुपेत्यैतं प्रश्नमपृच्छत । षोडशकलं भारद्वाज पुरुषं वेत्थ तमहं कुमारमब्रुवं

नाहमिमं वेद यद्यहमिममवेदिषं कथं ते नावक्ष्यमिति समूलो वा एष

परिशुष्यति योऽनृतमभिवदति तस्मान्नार्हाम्यनृतं वक्तुं स तूष्णीं रथमारुह्य

प्रव्राज । तं त्वा पृच्छामि क्वासौ पुरुष इति ॥ ६.१

तस्मै स होवाच । इहैवान्तःशरीरे सोम्य स पुरुषो यस्मिन्नेताः षोडश कलाः

प्रभवन्तीति ॥ ६.२

स ईक्षांचक्रे । कस्मिन्नहमुत्क्रान्त उत्क्रान्तो भविष्यामि कस्मिन् वा प्रतिष्ठिते

प्रतिष्ठास्यामीति ॥ ६.३

स प्राणमसृजत प्राणाच्छ्रद्धां खं वायुर्ज्योतिरापः पृथिवीन्द्रियं मनः ।

अन्नमन्नाद् वीर्यं तपो मन्त्राः कर्मलोका लोकेषु च नाम च ॥ ६.४

स यथेमा नद्यः स्यन्दमानाः समुद्रायणाः समुद्रं प्राप्यास्तं गच्छन्ति भिद्येते

तासां नामरूपे समुद्र इत्येवं प्रोच्यते । एवमेवास्य परिद्रष्टुरिमाः षोडश कलाः

पुरुषायणाः पुरुषं प्राप्यास्तं गच्छन्ति भिद्येते चाऽऽसां नामरूपे पुरुष इत्येवं

प्रोच्यते स एषोऽकलोऽमृतो भवति तदेष श्लोकः ॥ ६.५

अरा इव रथनाभौ कला यस्मिन् प्रतिष्ठिताः ।

तं वेद्यं पुरुषं वेद यथा मा वो मृत्युः परिव्यथा इति ॥ ६.६

तान् होवाचैतावदेवाहमेतत्परं ब्रह्म वेद । नातः परमस्तीति ॥ ६.७

ते तमर्चयन्तस्त्वं हि नः पिता योऽस्माकमविद्यायाः परं पारं तारयसीति ।

नमः परमऋषिभ्यो नमः परमऋषिभ्यः ॥ ६.८

<u>॥ इति प्रश्नोपनिषत् समाप्ता ॥</u>

ॐ भद्रं कर्णेभिः शृणुयाम देवाः । भद्रं पश्येम माक्षभिर् यजत्राः । स्थिरैरङ्गैस् तुष्टुवाꣳ सस्तनूभिः । व्यशेम देवहितं यदायुः । स्वस्ति न इन्द्रो वृद्धश्रवाः । स्वस्ति नः पूषा विश्ववेदाः । स्वस्ति नस्ताक्ष्यों अरिष्टनेमिः । स्वस्ति नो बृहस्पतिर्दधातु ॥ ॐ शान्तिः शान्तिः शान्तिः ॥

# Sanskrit Grammar

Sandhis separated word by word पदच्छेद (प०),
Verses in prose order अन्वय (अ०),and with विभक्ति
Cases.

<u>Abbreviations</u>
Nouns

      **m** masculine, **f** feminine, **n** neuter; **V** vocative
      1/1 = vibhakti case from 1 to 7/number 1 to 3

Indeclinables (uninflected nouns or verbs) **0**
In Sanskrit the **adverbs** are mostly uninflected.

Verbs

      iii/1 = person i to iii / number 1 to 3
      **PPP** = Past Participle Passive = क्त
      **PPA** = Past Participle Active = क्तवत्
      **PrPA** = PresentParticiple Active = शतृ/ शानच्
      **PoPP** = PotentialParticiple Passive = य, तव्य,
      अनीयर् (gerund)
      तुमुन् = infinitive, in the sense of "to do"

Anusvara and Makara have been kept as they are in
Padacheda, to avoid over work. E.g. इदं should be
written as इदम् in Padacheda.

Sanskrit Literature frequently omits the verb – "is".
The words भवति,  अस्ति  etc. are implicit.

E.g. तदेष श्लोकः ॥ ११.० = तदेष श्लोकः भवति ॥

Since Sanskrit is an inflectional language, the **spelling of the same word** changes as per context or usage. Hence words can be **placed anywhere** in a sentence, as in poetic use, without change in meaning. The matrix shows how.

## Verb inflections in Sanskrit – a sample chart

| 982 गम्ऌ गतौ – to go, also in the sense of attainment | | | |
|---|---|---|---|
| Present Tense Active voice लट् कर्त्तरि प्रयोग: | | | |
| Person/no | singular | dual | plural |
| Third | गच्छति[iii/1] | गच्छत:[iii/2] | गच्छन्ति[iii/3] |
| Second | गच्छसि[ii/1] | गच्छथ:[ii/2] | गच्छथ [ii/3] |
| First | गच्छामि[i/1] | गच्छाव:[i/2] | गच्छाम:[i/3] |

## Noun declensions in Sanskrit – a sample chart

| Masculine stem, vowel अ ending | | | |
|---|---|---|---|
| (र्–आ–म्–अ) राम[iii] Lord's name | | | |
| | singular[1] | dual[2] | plural[3] |
| 1 Doer | राम:[1/1] | रामौ[1/2] | रामा:[1/3] |
| 2 Object | रामम्[2/1] | रामौ[2/2] | रामान्[2/3] |
| 3 by | रामेण[3/1] | रामाभ्याम्[3/2] | रामै:[3/3] |
| 4 for | रामाय[4/1] | रामाभ्याम्[4/2] | रामेभ्य:[4/3] |
| 5 from | रामात्[5/1] | रामाभ्याम्[5/2] | रामेभ्य:[5/3] |
| 6 of | रामस्य[6/1] | रामयो:[6/2] | रामाणाम्[6/3] |
| 7 in | रामे[7/1] | रामयो:[7/2] | रामेषु[7/3] |
| Vocative | हे राम[V/1] | हे रामौ[V/2] | हे रामा:[V/3] |

| Masculine stem, consonant त् ending | | |
| --- | --- | --- |
| मरुत्[m] Wind, Breeze, Air | | |
| | singular[1] | dual[2] | plural[3] |
| 1 Doer | मरुत् [1/1] | मरुतौ [1/2] | मरुतः [1/3] |
| 2 Object | मरुतम् [2/1] | मरुतौ [2/2] | मरुतः [2/3] |
| 3 by | मरुता [3/1] | मरुद्भ्याम् [3/2] | मरुद्भिः [3/3] |
| 4 for | मरुते [4/1] | मरुद्भ्याम् [4/2] | मरुद्भ्यः [4/3] |
| 5 from | मरुतः [5/1] | मरुद्भ्याम् [5/2] | मरुद्भ्यः [5/3] |
| 6 of | मरुतः [6/1] | मरुतोः [6/2] | मरुताम् [6/3] |
| 7 in | मरुति [7/1] | मरुतोः [7/2] | मरुत्सु [7/3] |
| Vocative | हे मरुत् [V/1] | हे मरुतौ [V/2] | हे मरुतः [V/3] |

## Moods and Tenses in Sanskrit

| 1 | लट् | Present Tense |
| --- | --- | --- |
| 2 | लुङ् | Aorist Past Tense, *before from now onwards* |
| 3 | लङ् | Imperfect Past Tense – *before from yesterday onwards* |
| 4 | लिट् | Perfect Past Tense – *distant unseen past* |
| 5 | लृट् | Simple Future Tense – *now onwards* |
| 6 | लुट् | Periphrastic Future Tense – *tomorrow onwards* |
| 7 | लृङ् | Conditional Mood - *if/then in past or future* |
| 8 | लोट् | Imperative Mood – *request* |
| 9 | विधि– लिङ् | Potential Mood – *order* विधिलिङ् (also known as Optative Mood) |
| 10 | आशीर्– लिङ् | Benedictive Mood – *blessing* आशीर्लिङ् (also used in the sense of a curse) |

# Conjugation process of Verb

वदन्ति = they say, they describe.

1st conjugation Root, Parasmaipadi.

1009 √ वदँ व्यक्तायां वाचि । to tell, relate, describe.

1.3.1 भूवादयो धातवः। वदँ = वद्अँ ।

1.3.2 उपदेशोऽजनुनासिक इत्। 1.3.9 तस्य लोपः। वद् ।

3.4.69 लः कर्मणि च भावे चाकर्मकेभ्यः। वद् ।

3.2.123 वर्तमाने लट्। 3.4.77 लस्य । वद् + लँट् ।

1.3.3 हलन्त्यम् । 1.3.9 तस्य लोपः । वद्+लँ ।

1.3.2 उपदेशोऽजनुनासिक इत् । 1.3.9तस्य लोपः । वद्+ल् ।

3.4.78 तिप्तस्झिसिप्थस्थमिब्वस्मस् तातांझथासाथांध्वमिड्वहिमहिङ् ।

1.4.199 लः परस्मैपदम् । choose Parasmaipada affix.

वद्+झि । we are conjugating third person

1.4.101 तिङस्त्रीणि त्रीणि प्रथममध्यमोत्तमाः ।

1.4.102 तान्येकवचनद्विवचनबहुवचनान्येकशः । वद्+झि । plural

1.4.108 शेषे प्रथमः । वद्+झि । this is called "प्रथमः" i.e. the **first and most** used in language, third person.

3.4.113 तिङ्शित्सार्वधातुकम् । वद्+झि ।

3.1.68 कर्त्तरि शप् । वद्+शप्+झि ।

3.4.113तिङ्शित्सार्वधातुकम् । वद्+शप्+झि ।

7.1.3 झोऽन्तः । वद्+शप्+ अन्ति ।

1.3.3 हलन्त्यम्। 1.3.8लशक्वतद्धिते। 1.3.9तस्य लोपः।वद्+अ+अन्ति ।

6.1.97 अतो गुणे । वद्+अन्ति । sandhi drops the अकारः ।

8.3.24 नश्वापदान्तस्य झलि । वद् + अंति । Anusvara appears

8.4.58 अनुस्वारस्य ययि परसवर्णः । वद् + अन्ति ।

Anusvara again changes to नकारः ।

वद् + अन्ति = वदन्ति [iii/3] लट् । iii = 3$^{rd}$ person, 3 = plural.

Third person plural, Present Tense.

# Declension process of Noun

ब्रह्म = Brahma. The Lord. Highest Intelligence.

Stem Brahman ब्रह्मन् n $\longrightarrow$ ब्रह्म neuter Nominative [1/1]

The Great Lord. The Invisible presence.

1.2.45 अर्थवदधातुरप्रत्ययः प्रातिपदिकम् । ब्रह्मन्

1.2.46 कृत्तद्धितसमासाश्च । 3.1.1 प्रत्ययः । 3.1.2 परश्च ।

4.1.1 ङ्याप्प्रातिपदिकात् । 4.1.2 स्वौजस-

मौट्छष्टाभ्याम्भिस्ङेभ्याम्भ्यस्ङसिभ्याम्भ्यस्ङसोसाम्ङ्योस्सुप् ।

1.4.104 विभक्तिश्च । 1.4.103 सुपः = use one of these

vibhakti suffix. ब्रह्मन् + सुँ ।

1.4.22 द्व्येकयोर्द्विवचनैकवचने = singular number taken.

ब्रह्मन् + सुँ ।

7.1.23 स्वमोर्नपुंसकात् । 2.4.13 यस्मात्प्रत्ययविधिस्तदादि

प्रत्ययेऽङ्गम् । 6.4.1 अङ्गस्य । [1]st and [2]nd case Vibhakti

drops for neuter stem. ब्रह्मन् ।

1.4.17 स्वादिष्वसर्वनामस्थाने । The word gets पदसंज्ञा ।

ब्रह्मन् ।

8.2.7 न लोपः प्रातिपदिकान्तस्य । Final नकार drops.

ब्रह्म [n1/1] ।

*Neuter. First case nominative singular.* **Brahma.**
The Highest. The Supreme. Shiva. Purusha. Tao.
The Beautiful, The Love, The Infinite, The Divine.
Any name is **Him.**
All directions point to **It.** Every form is **She.**

# References

https://www.ashtangayoga.info/philosophy/sanskrit-and-devanagari/transliteration-tool/
http://spokensanskrit.org/        https://upanishads.org.in/
Audio Chant
http://vedicheritage.gov.in/upanishads/prashnopanishad/
https://www.youtube.com/watch?v=TDfS7gy1SxQ
https://www.youtube.com/watch?v=EFv_sUuzBYY

Guided Meditations Sri Sri Ravi Shankar
https://www.youtube.com/playlist?list=PL480C9CCB94DF5D82
Sitarama Sastri – Katha and Prasna Upanishads Vol 2 – 1st – 1928 - V. C. Seshacharri, Madras.

Swami Sarvananda – Prasna Upanishad – 1st – 1922 - Sri Ramakrishna Math, Madras. (also kindle eBook)

Gita Press – प्रश्नोपनिषद् सानुवाद शाङ्करभाष्यसहित – 1st - 1936 – Gita Press, Gorakhpur.

Kshemkarandass Trivedi गोपथब्राह्मणभाष्यम् – 1st 2008 Chaukhamba Sanskrit Pratishthan, Delhi.

KLV Sastry & Anantarama Sastri – Sabda Manjari 1961– Reprint - 2013 – RS Vadhyar & Sons, Palghat.

Swami Devarupananda – मन्त्रपुष्यम् - 4th – 2010 – Ramakrishna Math, Khar, Mumbai.

Swami Paramarthananda – Prasna Upanishad Discourse – 1st – 2016 – Arsha Avinash Foundation, Coimbatore.

Sri Sri Ravi Shankar - Upanishad Vol1 - Ishavasya Kena Katha Yogasara - 1st – 2017 – Sri Sri Publications Trust, Bangalore

Ashwini Kumar Aggarwal – Dhatupatha of Panini – 2nd – 2017 – Devotees of Sri Sri Ravi  Shankar Ashram, Punjab.

# Epilogue

It is a great time, the Master has arrived, and he is there to enlighten, bless, and give eternal happiness.

The Meditations on OM are simple, highly effective, and easily obtained in today's world on mobile phones and laptops through the internet.

It is time to welcome Divinity in the form of OM. Just make it a daily ritual in a familiar and friendly manner and reap manifold joys.

सर्वे भवन्तु सुखिनः । सर्वे सन्तु निरामयाः ।

सर्वे भद्राणि पश्यन्तु । मा कश्चिद् दुःख भाग्भवेत् ॥

ॐ शान्तिः शान्तिः शान्तिः ॥

When faith has blossomed in life,
Every step is led by the Divine.

Sri Sri Ravi Shankar

**Om Namah Shivaya**

जय गुरुदेव

www.ingramcontent.com/pod-product-compliance
Lightning Source LLC
LaVergne TN
LVHW051534170726
843492LV00006B/1767